TONI AKERS

Recognize

Confronting the demonic forces
that control our lives

In Time Publishing & Media Group
150 North Wacker Drive
Chicago, Il 60601

Visit our website at *www.intimepublishing.com*

Printed in the United States of America

First Print Edition

Toni Akers
Recognize: Confronting the demonic forces that
control our lives

ISBN# 0-9746384-7-1

For more information on Toni Akers:

www.toniakers.com

P.O Box 458, Bollingbrook, Il 60440

RECOGNIZE is your key to understanding your life and the forces that can sometimes work against you. If you have experienced feelings of rejection, hatred, poverty, bad relationships or drugs, you must RECOGNIZE that you have an enemy who is very real, and who will stop at nothing to destroy you. There is, however, something you can do to turn your life around but until you RECOGNIZE you will continue to just about keep your head above water. Today is your day to RECOGNIZE.

Dedication

This book is dedicated to my mother. Mom, I thank
you for sending me to church and making it a point that I
get to know God. You are a loving and giving person and I
know that God doesn't make mistakes. You are my
mother and I will always love
and honor you.

Table of Contents

Acknowledgments

I first want to thank Jesus Christ for dying on the cross for me and giving me the right to the key of eternal life, and the courage to write this book. I dedicate this book to my Lord and Savior because He is my Deliverer and my Comforter. Through His blood I have the authority to escape the power of darkness that was designed to destroy me.

I would also like to thank my family, and my husband Rudy Akers, for being there for me and my two beautiful children Ajani and Marque.

My Pastor and friend, Dr. William H. Samuel, I thank you. You motivated me and assisted me in many ways in bringing this book to life. I also want to thank Congressman Danny Davis who is someone I highly respect and admire. He has a great understanding of inner city issues and a sincere desire to make positive changes in the community.

I have an entire list of mentors and teachers who've helped me mature in my walk with Christ. My Grandmother "Sister Miller", Pastor Campbell, Apostle Anthony Earl, Mother Dorothy Clark, Sister Anne Smith, Apostle Anna Poplous, and two godly men whom I've never met in person, but have inspired me through their books and workshops Bishop T.D. Jakes and Apostle John Eckhardt.

I can't forget my sisters, especially Crystal Maghett-Brunson, whom has always been there for me. I love her for her support and courage. My many friends, especially Frieda McKinnon and Deirdre Taylor. Frieda said for years, "You should write a book. People would not believe many of the things you've suffered and experienced in life. Write a book, it will help others know that God is real." And Deirdre who spent time with me editing along with Mario McGowan.

I've overcome many obstacles not by my own power, but by the power of the Holy Spirit. I stand on Isaiah 61, "The Spirit of the Lord God is upon me. Because the Lord has anointed me to preach good tidings to the poor, He has sent me to heal the brokenhearted. To proclaim liberty to the captives, and the opening of the prison to those who are bound..."

- Rev. Toni Akers

Preface

This book is being written for anyone seeking or wanting to know God. Living and watching others die in the streets or maybe even people who have suffered many different hardships may give a person the impression that God doesn't exist, but He is just as real today as he was 2000 years ago. I don't care what you are going through, Jesus can deliver. You better recognize!

If you are a church leader who's looking to grow the church and to be a Nation inside of a Nation, you better recognize that while you are building and laying bricks for a firm foundation, the adversary is right along side of you trying to remove each brick as fast as you lay them, so as you walk this good walk of faith it would be wise to recognize and discern every spiritual activity within and around your church (your territory). We can't be so heavenly minded that we are no earthly good. The devil operates in the simple things in life and we need to stay focused and in the spiritual mix to make a difference.

You, who are a believer and believe that believing is enough—the rest of that church stuff is a waste, and for you, who are playing church, let me let you in on a secret—the devil don't like you, and he is waiting for a time that he can devour you. You Better Recognize that while we are here on this nice green earth, there is a spiritual fight going on all around us. The challenge, If You Choose to Take It, is to sharpen your spiritual sword, and open your eyes and see what you ain't been seeing—not because you don't have eyes to see, but because you just don't RECOGNIZE!

Introduction

Could any good thing come out of Lawndale? What is the story of this petite princess from Chicago's Westside with the power of the Lord's presence? She grew up to be a powerful minister, but what did she face along the way? Why is she able to Recognize the adversary when others just seem to look at things as if people are simply acting out or just plain foolish? Before we go back in time, let's look at what is happening now.

A thirteen year-old girl stood defiantly in front of a traditional church congregation. Her arms showed the marks of attempted suicide and her wild, nappy hair signified she had long since given up on concern for how she looked. She was angry at the world, her mother, the church and God.

She had joined a group called the "Gothics" where she learned that Satan understood her anger. Red and black-the color of blood and death signified her mood. Pain is pleasure, hate is love, and misery is joy are the precepts they taught.

Relief could come if she would only cut herself, curse her family and run away from this miserable world. Her world was now hiding under porches, sleeping in allies, and finding food in garbage cans. After all, pain, death and destruction had now become relief and only God was standing in the way of the long awaited eternal torture with Satan.

The Pastor signaled for his new Assistant (Toni) to come forth to pray for this young girl. She obediently stepped forward and began to peer deep into the eyes of this defiant teenager. The congregation was in awe as the Assistant said a prayer as she probed the defiant teen. Her stance indicated that she "recognized" the symptoms of the young girl and was in no way surprised at this nasty enemy which seemed to now possess the being of the little girl. The Assistant Pastor's appearance seemed a contradiction to the warrior which was about to emerge. The clear eyes, petite build and deceptive smile did not give an indication of the powerful presence which was about to emerge.

"Satan", she screamed with power and authority, you cannot have this child. I rebuke you in the name of Jesus!" The Westside Warrior said, "Furthermore I command that you loose this girl and I send you to the dry places where you belong. You must go! I command you in the Name of Jesus!" Toni continued.

After 15 minutes of this kind of warfare, the stunned teen staggered, cried and then submitted to the powerful presence of the Lord. The congregation and the girl were collectively shocked by the newly ordained preacher whose reputation as a "beauty queen" and perhaps a pampered "pretty girl" had any such connection with such awesome power!

What was the traditional congregation witnessing? Where did this woman get such strength? Was this some new form of religion? After all, the congregation wondered was this not the 21st Century where demons, witches, warlocks and such had long since been dismissed. I ask again, could any good thing come out of Lawndale? What is the story of this petite princess from Chicago's Westside with the power of the Lord's presence?

Pastor Doctor William H. Samuels

To the reader of this book

Most people do not like to talk about demons. They prefer to say things like, "the devil made me do it", or "something made me do that." Even better, "a feeling came over me and all of a sudden," but the reality of it is that there is a force called the adversary who is constantly roaring about seeking someone to devour. First, we need to recognize that this force exists and then we need to submit to God, resist the devil and he will flee from us. We need to also recognize that the phrase "unclean spirits" appears throughout the Bible. We tend to think that it's some ugly creature that is too horrible for us to look at, but when you see a loved one with blood shot eyes from alcohol or drugs, that's an unclean spirit; or a sex crazed person who lacks moral wisdom or judgment. That's an unclean spirit! A mother who hates her daughter or a father who hates his son. Now, let's get this clear. Everything can't be blamed on the devil. We have our own free will, and many of our circumstances and conditions are blamed on Satan and his team of demons, but in reality it is really just us. However, when we start to recognize the real forms in which the adversary is disguising himself, we will be able to use our faith and our God given authority over these demonic forces and demand them to leave us alone.

I grew up in an area where violence was a normal activity. This area is called the Lawndale Community located on the Westside of Chicago. Lawndale was and still is one of the highest crime areas in the nation. Murder, daily fights, people cursing out one another, gun shots, someone running down the street trying to get away with a free bag of chips or running from the police after bailing out of a stolen car are regular occurrences. Everyone else is simply making sure they do not cross into some other gang's territory because that meant death or a royal beat down. The street life was the real game of life for me. Every move on the "board of life" was very crucial. Getting ready for school in the morning was more than just checking to make sure that my homework was in my book bag, but also checking to make sure that I had my switch blade and brass knuckles because I never knew when a gang of girls would roll up on me and try to take my clothes and/or shoes. This lifestyle may have appeared normal for some, but I started to recognize that there was an invisible force on this earth that was trying to control the minds and hearts of the people. I started to recognize that it was more than just gang warfare, poverty warfare, sexual immorality warfare, single parenting warfare, sickness and disease warfare, but it was all out bloody, ungodly Spiritual Warfare. It was really more about what spirits were operating in the atmosphere and which demons felt that they had a right to be in my territory.

I am reminded of the story of Little Red Riding Hood. She went over the river and through the woods to her grandmother's house, but when she got there, she noticed something different about grandmother. Her grandmother had bigger teeth, bigger ears, bigger feet, but Little Red Riding Hood did not want to believe that this wolf wasn't her grandmother. This is the way we operate in life a lot of times. We look at our loved ones, and don't want to believe that something has gotten a hold of them. We simply say things like, "they're just tripping or that person is just acting crazy." We never stop to think that the adversary has taken up residence within this person and is having his way with the host (the person in question). Now this may sound a little far fetched for those of you who don't believe in demons, or do not believe that Christians can be possessed by a demon, but keep on living and sharpening your spiritual eye, and you'll begin to see more than what meets the naked eye. You will start to recognize that you are dealing with demonic spirits more often than not. You see, I learned at an early age that Jesus is Emmanuel (God is with us). He is Omnipresent, meaning He is with you always. When I relate this to the way a street gang operates, they need back-up when they are faced with two or three people trying to jump them. You see, the adversary, Satan is always trying to jump us and our backup is Jesus; but we need to recognize what type of fight we are in and we need to know how to call on the name of Jesus. We cannot afford to not have this type of knowledge because without it the people will perish. Ephesians 6:11 talks about putting on the full armor of God. Ephesians also points out that we do not fight against flesh and blood, but against the rulers, against the powers, against the world forces of darkness, against the spiritual forces of wickedness in the heavenly places. Many people don't realize that there is more than one heaven. There are three layers to the heavenlies, and when Paul speaks of wickedness in the heavenly places found in Ephesians 4:9-10 he is not talking about the place where our Lord and Savior resides, but he is talking about the 1st heaven where Satan resides.

What you are about to read is a true story about my life. It was day to day living, but there was an ungodly strategy that was designed to devour me, get me off my course and to make me lose faith in God. Demons are real and they can hide in the flesh. Many of the outcomes will show little victory and it wasn't because my God wasn't able. It was because of my lack of knowledge in His ability. As I grew up

Recognize

and learned more about Spiritual Warfare, I learned how to stop the devil in his tracks before he could roll up on me. I learned how to release angels and God's blessings in the atmosphere to keep a hedge of protection around me. I learned how to decree that "no weapon formed against me would prosper and every tongue that would rise up against me in judgment would be condemned." I learned how to call on the name of the Lord. It's not complicated. We all have the power to speak things and rebuke things. We don't have to walk around in fear thinking that Satan is going to get us. We just need to recognize that he exists and we do have weapons of warfare to deal with him when he shows up. **Get ready to recognize.**

The Good, the Bad, and the Ugly

As a young girl growing up on Chicago's Westside, I felt like I was growing up in Vietnam during the war. Every block was like a war zone. Everybody knew somebody who had been shot or killed. Living with this reality, I started to accept the idea of an early death. I felt at the age of 9 that if I lived to be 30 I would have made it past the average age of death in the hood. While the life expectancy for men and women nationwide is in the mid-seventies, in the "hood" death came suddenly.

Now, my parents and my grandmother played a major role in shaping my views and outlook on life. Their teachings, whether intentional or unintentional, helped shaped the woman I am today.

My mom and dad lived in two separate worlds and my grandmother was a church going, praying woman. Because of this, I started to recognize what I call "the good, the bad and the ugly." As I grew up, I soon recognized that these adjectives were words that could be used to describe demonic spirits. I became aware that even though many desired to be good, there were controlling spirits in their lives that caused them to be "bad and ugly." But in Rom 8:1-2 it talks about how there is no condemnation to those who are in Christ Jesus, who do not walk according to the flesh, but walk according to the Spirit....... how Christ Jesus has made us free from the law of sin and death. It's because of this passage of scripture that I am alive today to share my story with you.

23

Recognize

Meet Mom

My mother was a very strong and determined woman. She was always at home cooking and cleaning. My dad, on the other hand, was always "in the streets," as she put it. She would cook, clean and make sure our homework was done and then play the waiting game for my dad to get home. Once he made it in, our quiet apartment would turn into a loud shouting, yelling, cursing arena with objects smashing into the walls and floors. My sisters, brothers and I never really knew what all the shouting and yelling was all about, but we would keep score on who was winning. My dad won most of the battles, but my mom had the most points in cursing and name-calling.

All we knew was that mommy was mad at daddy. She was always mad at him and he was always gone. My mom was always at home dealing with her seven kids while my dad was out "kicking it" with the boys. I would try to stay out of mom's way because she always appeared irritated and on edge. I knew it was because her husband wasn't what she wanted him to be. She was always sad and there was nothing I could do about it. There was nothing any of us could do about it. We would always say, "If daddy comes in here drunk again and tries to hit mommy, we should all get up and jump him." In our hearts we knew that we were too young to take on a grown man, but we didn't want to see mom get hurt. We began to recognize two things—first, that we were just helpless in this painful domestic war and second, what I later learned to call demons were in operation in our home.

Sundays were a day of rest for my mother. She would

Recognize

wake us all up and make us walk to a nearby church where my Grandmother taught Sunday school. For some reason my mother didn't like going to church. We all just figured that Sundays were the only day for her to catch up on her rest. Watching my mother struggle so hard made me determined at an early age to never get married and to never have kids. Our family wasn't like the families I watched on TV. There was no Brady Bunch here! My mother worked hard to keep the family fed, clothed and happy. My dad did little to pitch in. Every now and then, however, my dad would do the right thing. I remember times when we all went to places like Fun Town and Adventure Land.

When my dad was taking care of business like this, it made my mom happy. But something had a hold on my dad. He could never stay consistent. My mom had a lot to deal with and I often wished that I was old enough to get a job to help her pay the bills. When the bills were paid and all was well, my mom was happy—and I liked seeing her happy. I have learned to respect her over the years as I've learned that the women of today are not made of the same material as the women of yesteryear. I can honestly say I would feel a little hard pressed trying to raise seven kids by myself, while spending a lot of the time dealing with a man who was only around "every blue moon."

I often felt rejected by my mom perhaps because she felt rejected herself, and was being hindered by the trials of life. She was always in pain emotionally, so she gave only what she had to give. The sad thing about this is that my mom had a lot of love to give, I think, deep down inside. She just could not reach deep enough to get it. I just couldn't help but think that the man that she once loved just brought out the worst in her. Not recognizing that a spirit of rejection had moved in and made himself at home, I found out the hard way that the saying "misery loves company" is true. I remember getting such harsh treatment from my mother that often made me want to burn down half of Chicago. Galatians 3:1 talks about being bewitched. Any person not believing and living the life of Christ through faith may have possibly been bewitched.

My mother recruited me into her misery. I remember feeling the hatred, the pressure, and the oppression of living and identifying with a rejected wife and a mother drained of her love.

My mother became contaminated by betrayal and abandonment which turned into rejection and bitterness. These evil spirits were able to make their strongholds into my mother's life by way of emotional trauma. When bitterness is planted in a person's heart it begins to eat away at the love that's in their heart and begins to take over. As a result, a person is not able to love and is trapped in his or her own cage that is guarded by Satan himself. My mother has the gift of love and had shown it on many occasions throughout her life, but Satan's strategy was to steal it away from her. The adversary doesn't want any of us showing our love to anyone. It is totally against what he's about. If he could overtake her with bitterness, then His destructive plan would filter right down to her seven children in one form or another. This is truly a spiritual fight. The fight is still on and we need to work on taking back what he has stolen from many of us; and that is a mother's love.

Recognize

A PRAYER
FOR ALL HURTING MOTHERS

Lord God, I believe by faith that this book was written for me. I pray right now that You heal me of all of my disappointments, my loneliness, and my lack of faith; that I'd be able to do all things through Your love, even become a better mother. Lord I pray that You would heal my broken heart, and give me back all of the pieces of my soul. Father God I pray for total restoration in my mind, emotions and will. I pray that I begin to walk in wisdom, and start to view each of my children as a gift from You God and not a mistake. Lord, build me up where I am torn down, and return to me what Satan has stolen. I come against bitterness and anger, and I pray that joy, peace and love will be my portion on today, and that I will walk in victory from this day forward. IN JESUS NAME I PRAY, AMEN

Meet the Magic Man

Although my dad may have not been a great husband to my mother, he was certainly a cool guy to hang out with. My dad favored me a lot and did more for me than any of my other brothers and sisters. At least, this is what everyone would say. He would let me hang out with him almost every Saturday. This was a bittersweet situation for my mom. She knew that my father would have me around some questionable people, but she also recognized that I could also be her personal spy.

My dad worked as a laborer during the week, and on the weekends worked in his aunt's liquor store. His mom died when he was only two years old and, in a sense, his aunt was the only mom he ever knew. My great aunt's liquor store was always full of some very interesting people. Most of them looked like death on a stick. Many of them had no teeth, bad odors, uncombed hair and thin body form. Others were ashy and wrinkled. My dad would let me sit behind the bar and help him serve the people. I could not sell any of the liquor; however, I could sell the juices that were in the cooler or the chips, which came in a variety of flavors. At the age of 10, I felt proud to be able to help out.

People always came into the liquor store begging and pleading. Some would be begging for liquor on credit, and others would be pleading for a free drink and stuff. The "stuff" represented things which people would discuss with my father over to the side. Even though my father gave me these early business experiences, he was very protective of me at times. He would go into a rage on any customer that

29

Recognize

would say certain things in front of me. So, to keep things "on the down low," some of his regular customers would stick their head in the door and say "Magic Man, can I speak to you for a minute?" I'd always wonder what those frequent mini-meetings were all about. Yes, my dad's street name was "Magic Man." The "Magic Man" was always handling some secret business. I would watch him from a distance as he conversed with some very shady looking people. Once the deal was done, and money would switch hands, he would come back behind the bar and say, "How is my favorite girl doing?" Whatever the deal was, he would be in a much happier, playful mood upon completion.

Now the liquor store was always full of smoke, loud music, and people from all levels of income. Some customers would try to use food stamps to buy liquor, and others would be peeling off 20's, 50's and 100 dollar bills. The people who looked like they had a little money would come over to the bar, buy a few shots of hard liquor, and disappear behind this thick beaded curtain toward the back of the store. I was never allowed back there. As people would travel in and out of the store, and from behind the curtain, I would watch them and wonder what these people had in common. They all looked so different; but in a strange way, they all looked the same.

Some of the customers would come in and slide me a few dollar bills for my pocket and others would come in asking if I could spare a dollar. Then there were those who were banned from coming into the store. When my dad or aunt saw anyone that had been banned from coming to the liquor store, they would yell at them as if they were chasing away a stray dog, "Get your @#$%& away from here right now!".

Sometimes both my dad and aunt would say this in unison. Well, it's time for my dad to take me home now. He knows that my mom would be getting me up bright and early for Sunday school.

I felt sad for the people buying liquor. They would hand over their last penny and reach for the liquor as if they were filling a prescription. As if, the substance in that brown paper bag would make it all better. I was young, but I knew that their habit of drinking was only a temporary fix. They all needed something more. Something to take the pain away. I was able to recognize the pain by simply looking them in the eyes. I didn't recognize it at the time, but soon enough I realized that I was looking at the demon of addiction.

Demons were on assignment to destroy my dad. He operated in adultery as many men did, and he had an addiction to alcohol. The devil tricked him and many others who drank into thinking that the answer was in the bottle and not in God. Many of the people at the liquor store didn't even know that God was able to deliver them and free them from their addiction. Many people think that their hope and deliverance can be found in a little brown paper bag. But in Matthew 17 starting at the 14th verse it talks about a boy possessed with demons and the disciples of the Lord were unable to cast the demons out. Jesus called them a faithless and a perverse generation, but as you read down to the 20th verse he says that if we have faith the size of a mustard seed we would be able to speak to a mountain and to tell it to move and it will.

Recognize

Meet Mary

Mary was one of the people not allowed in the liquor store. I once learned about a "Mary" in one of my grandmother's Sunday school lessons. This Mary, however, was not the same. This Mary was very ugly to look at. She was skinny like a skeleton with wrinkled ashy skin. She had red eyes, where the white was supposed to be. She had on clothes that were ripped, dirty, stained, and looked like they needed to be in the garbage. She could never walk straight due to her drunkenness, and she would always be saying curse words to the sky. In short, she was crazy. We called her the crazy lady. One day my dad had to make a quick run and told me to stay at the store with my aunt. My aunt needed to make a quick run upstairs to use the bathroom. She told me to tell her customers that she would be right back down. Business was a little slow and I felt like a big girl being able to hold the fort down by myself. I looked down for just a quick moment, and as I looked up I saw Mary halfway in the store. She walked over to me, and I just froze. I didn't move or say a word as she approached me. This was the first time I saw Mary up close. She was just as ugly as I thought, but, to my surprise, she had a sweet spirit that was deep, deep, deep down inside. I was able to recognize that there were two sides to Mary, as I looked her in the eye. It almost appeared that she didn't want to be in the body that she was in. She smiled in my face with her bald mouth, and said, "Hey pretty girl." Her voice sounded like a man's voice with a bad cold. "Can you do an old lady a favor and give her something to drink?" Her breath was hot, and it smelled like the contents of a sewer. I was surprised that I wasn't afraid of her. I suddenly realized that she was not that old, just sick.

Recognize

I looked around for a clean glass and asked her what she wanted. She pointed to something that looked like water, and I took it off the shelf and poured it in a glass. Before I could hand it to her, she snatched it, and swallowed it like it was a cold glass of water. Afterwards, she opened her eyes and she had a look on her face as if I had given her a million bucks. She could hear my aunt returning so she took off as quickly as possible.

I began to pray and ask God to never let me be like that. My Grandmother would always tell me that you never know how your life is going to turn out. I figured if God was passing out virtues, I didn't want to end up like that drunken old lady.

I began to wonder if the church could help Mary-- I really wasn't sure. Drunken people would walk into the church all the time and the deacon (which to me was another name for bodyguard) would put them out right away.

I started to recognize that some of the people in the liquor store were good people. They just needed help. Some of them were even pleasant when they were not intoxicated. I even asked one lady why did she drink, and she told me that it was the only thing that took the pain away. As she walked away, I was thinking, what pain? Hey wait a minute, what pain?

When I returned home and was done answering my mother's questions, I would lie down and wonder how and why people became alcoholics. When I closed my eyes, I could still see the looks on so many of the people's faces from the liquor store. I could never get out of my mind the look on Mary's face as I reached for that clear liquid. And what about the lady who told me that liquor takes the pain away?

Now there were some customers in the store who were not looking for liquor. Some customers were looking to buy other "goods." They would be looking crazy and asking if I knew where the Magic Man was. I started to recognize that all of my dad's frequent mini meetings were with all of the drug-addicted people.

Life started to put a bad taste in my month. Where was my life leading? Would I get married like mom to a terrible man? Would I become hooked on a controlled substance? Maybe get shot in a drive-by. This was life on the wild, wild, Westside. This was the hand I was dealt.

Then I would wonder, what did I need to do to get God to like me enough to let me live a happy life? How do I get to know God? How can I help the people who are hurting? I began to ask questions that were too big for me to answer. As a result I would just fall asleep and anticipate hanging out with my dad next weekend. After all, that was the fun part. My dad always had jokes! These jokes would relieve my own pain.

One Saturday, the liquor store was really busy. I was even selling liquor to some of the customers. I was well trained on what to do if the cops came in the store. The funny thing was that the cops were some of the regular customers. One evening time passed so quickly that my dad didn't have time to take me home. So I stayed at the store all night "kicking it with the big dogs." I had no idea that the liquor store turned into a party joint at night. I started to get bored and wanted to know what was so great about liquor and why people bought it so often. Some seemed so

Recognize

happy after a few drinks while others said that it took the pain away. In addition, some women were even willing to sell their bodies for it. One lady offered to perform a sexual act for my dad for some liquor. She made this proposition right in front of me and my dad snapped off! I felt really sorry for her in more ways than one. My dad kicked her out of the store, and told her never to come back. I put my head down as if I didn't hear what the woman had said.

As I look back on many of the things that went on in that liquor store, I was surrounded by poverty, greed, perversion, addiction, foolishness, anger, and depression. There were people who just simply didn't want to be part of the life they were living, but they were trapped. They were dancing with suicide.

While the party was kicking off, and I was able to take a break, I decided to taste some of this great selling stuff. The clear watery looking stuff appeared to be the best seller. I decided to try it. I made a wish before I got started. You see, as a Disney lover, I didn't want this magic potion to turn me into some kind of ugly witch or worse, make me look like Mary. As a finicky eater, I decided to just stick my tongue in the stuff first just to get a feel for the flavor. I thought to myself, this would be on the safe side. I found a clean shot class, poured myself a shot and stuck my tongue in the glass.

"OH MY GOD! WHAT THE HELL IS THIS?" I remember asking myself. This has got to be what poison tastes like. I searched from my left to my right trying to remember which side of the bar they kept the water spray used when mixing drinks. I found it and used it to spray my tongue. My tongue was still burning when my dad walked up to me to see what I was up to. He asked me if I was getting tired. As he walked away, he said, "The next time you get thirsty, get a glass!" I was thinking, "the next time you need to get acid off of your car battery, use that clear liquid." Later on, I realized that clear liquid had a name, "vodka." I was so happy that drinking wasn't going to be a part of my future.

It's getting late, and now I'm ready to go home. My dad hasn't checked on me in a while. I wasn't supposed to go behind the forbidden curtain, but I was tired, and everyone that I would ask to tell my dad to come out would just disappear behind the curtain never to return. I finally built up enough nerve to go behind the curtain. I looked around for my dad for about two minutes while struggling to get my focus. The back room was darker and had more smoke than up front. I finally saw my dad. We looked eye to eye, and the look on his face was a look of surprise and shame, and the look on my face was that of disappointment. He had women hanging off of his arms while smoking something that did not look like a cigarette. I ducked back out of the curtain and was just mad! I saw a pool table with money on each end of the table, and I just knew that it was some serious stuff going on behind that curtain; drugs, gambling, and some level of sex.

It reminded me of a story I read in one of my bible story books, which gives the account of Moses returning from Mt. Sinai and finding the people partying and making a golden calf. I began to wonder if God saw us this way. I prayed and asked God not to make me like this. I didn't know I had choices.

Recognize

My dad eventually remarried. His wife was younger, but not pretty at all. I think the street life "did her in." In addition, she had the worst bags under her eyes. My dad became increasingly distant, and life wasn't the same. Every now and then my dad and I would hang out, but his new wife hated it. They would always argue about me. She felt that he would always put me first, and once again my dad was in domestic war. I didn't want my dad's life to be cramped due to me, so, sadly, I didn't visit him very much at all. I felt like the devil had snatched my dad away from me.

As influenced by Disney, I felt that my dad was now under the spell of some wicked witch. But the Holy Spirit continued to reveal to me that there are many demonic forces around us. Spiritual maturity allows us to recognize them and provide the power to dismiss them.

Mary not only had a spirit of addiction, but her addiction had a more aggressive driving force behind it; a spirit of suffering and hopelessness. She was trying to make her pain go away, but as a result she was creating more pain. She was killing herself and I'm sure that satan was pleased with her behavior. He was accomplishing his goal in that his mission was to kill and destroy her. I look back on stories like Mary's and many others and I feel like climbing on top of a mountain to shout "MY GOD IS ABLE TO DO EXCEEDINGLY, ABUNDANTLY, ABOVE THAT WHICH WE CAN ASK OR THINK!! He can even replace your brown paper bag if you could only become sober enough to recognize.

A PRAYER FOR ADDICTION

Father God, I come to You as humble as I know how, asking You to deliver me from my captivity. I am addicted to and want to be free. You said in Your Word that if I ask that it shall be given unto me if it's done in faith, so by faith I am asking that You take the taste of drugs, alcohol, _____, etc. from me right now in the mighty name of Jesus. I want to be a new creation in You Father. I no longer want to be bound by the lust of the flesh. I no longer want to be under a family curse. I no longer want to try and handle my life my way, but by Your way Father God. Help me LORD! Help me to walk away from sin, pain, and an early death. Help me to follow "You and Your ways. I believe that You are with me and that my life will never be the same after praying this prayer. By faith it is done. In Jesus Name, Amen.

Recognize

Meet my first Sunday School Teacher

It's Sunday! Time to go to church! Being out all night Saturday with my dad made it hard for me to go to church the next morning. Sundays were a day of rest for my mother, but not for me. Tired or not, I was going to church along with the rest of my brothers and sisters. For the most part, I really liked going to church. It was a day of bible stories, dressing up, singing, buying candy, and having fun. The quarter that my mother gave us to put in church, we spent it on candy.

My Grandmother (my mother's mother) was a member of a nearby Baptist Church for years. She had a big position in the church, and had a great rapport with the pastor and his wife. People would never call me by my name. I was Sister Miller's granddaughter. Needless to say, my grandmother was one of the "big dogs" in the church. She always wanted me to behave myself and took pride in studying my Sunday school lesson, so that I could get the answers right in class. This didn't happen very often, as I didn't like reading and didn't study the lesson too often. Amazingly enough I did learn a lot about the bible just by being in her class and listening to everyone interacting and talking about the bible stories. Not being in tune with the rest of the class I started recognizing that I was cramping my grandmother's style. Here she was a big time Sunday school teacher and her own granddaughter didn't know "jack" about the bible. I can remember those evil looks she would give me when I was sitting there not paying attention, chewing gum,

Recognize

and never able to answer any of the questions correctly. I believed that she really wanted me to disappear. I felt like I was under pressure, and I didn't like it. People expected more out of me because I was Sister Miller's granddaughter.

My best friend Frieda and I had signals that we came up with any time sister Miller would ask either of us a question. If she asked a question to either of us, and it was a question that we didn't know the answer to, the signal was to put your pointer finger up to your forehead as if we were in deep thought. While she was looking and waiting for the answer the other would shout out the correct answer. We were always helping each other out, but Sister Miller hated it when you spoke out of turn. Frieda and I stayed in trouble.

My grandmother was also an excellent seamstress. She made all of the choir robes for both the angelic and young adult choir. She was always busy doing work for the church. She even sang in the senior choir. Everyone in the church knew my grandmother, so I had to make sure that I wasn't one of the ones acting up in church. I felt that if God's eyes are in every place, I didn't want him to see me being bad. Being in the liquor store on Saturdays was bad enough. I was approaching 13, and I was told that once you become 13, you are responsible for your sins. Being 13 or older, and not saved would get you a one-way ticket to hell if you were to die. I felt that if I got the Ten Commandments "down-pat", then I should make it into the pearly gates.

When I turned 13 the world began to open up even wider for me. I started seeing and recognizing a lot of things around me. I started noticing boys. I had a love for fashion. I wanted to sing in the church choir, and I wanted to be a ballet dancer. My mother couldn't afford dance lessons or buy me the latest gear, but I took dance lessons at a nearby park district and my grandmother made me a lot of pretty outfits when I was acting right (as she puts it). She would always say, "You are a pretty girl, and you need to stop acting like a bad tail boy. If you keep showing out, I'm not going to make you anything else." I would look in the mirror at me in my new dress and say, "OK, grandma, I'm going to be good."

I couldn't wait until Sunday morning to wear my new dress. People would always ask me if Sister Miller made my dress, and I would say with great pride, "Yes, she did." I didn't take church that serious because the people were not that different from the people that hung out at the liquor store. The only difference was that they were dressed well and smelled better. Women would be in the ladies room talking and laughing about the sister that tried to sing some song, or discussing who was sleeping with whom. To me, they were more concerned about the way they looked on the outside and weren't doing much to improve the inside. The people at the liquor store were concerned about how they felt on the inside and weren't doing anything to improve the outside.

I started recognizing that I didn't want to be like the church folk either. They would always fight over what color they should wear for the choir's anniversary or who was going to lead songs this year. I would always see new faces during the choir's anniversary. I started to recognize that church was a place to show off your new clothing and talent, if you had either. Don't forget, it was also a place to find a husband or a wife.

Recognize

Some of the fights in the church were better than the fights at the liquor store. At the store, they would take the fight outside; fight, and then it was over in a matter of minutes. The next time you would see the two people involved in the fight together, they would be sharing a drink. But, baby," in the church," sometimes the fights would be right in the sanctuary (mostly verbal) with other church people urging on the conflict. These fights would last from one Sunday to the next. I would hurry to get to church to see and to hear the latest news. I wasn't going to church so much for God in those days. I was going to church because I had to. I'm not saying that I didn't love God, because I did. I just didn't think he was necessarily in the church.

During the week, I would read my bible storybooks that my grandmother gave me. They were better than the Sunday school booklets. I enjoyed the bible stories because they had lots of pictures. The stories were all tales of victory and how God smiles upon the children of Israel. I always wished that I were a child of God. I wanted to have favor with God. I didn't know how to get favor, and the people in the church weren't able to teach me. I began to want to know God the way the people in the bible knew Him. I wanted to experience the power that I read about. I wanted the power that God shared with Moses when he parted the Red Sea or the favor of Joseph as he gained control of Egypt. I wanted to share in the courage of David as he "kicked butt" for the cause of righteousness. He was winning all the battles not necessarily for himself, but in the name of the Lord.

I started wondering if the people of today could be victorious over drugs, alcohol and sexual sins. I wondered if they had the God of Moses, Abraham, Isaac and Jacob. Was

God still working things out for His people?

Church folk are just people off the street who decided one day to go to church; some have been transformed by the renewing of their minds and others haven't. Many are not necessarily sold out for the things of God. Therefore, don't be tricked into thinking that everyone that is in the church is God-fearing. You can run right into Satan, witch or a warlock at church, so you need to have on your full armor at all times. If you don't know what the full armor is, you better ask somebody. Being hurt in the church is most painful because it's unexpected. We must guard our heart, mind, and emotions at all times. Satan was kicked out of heaven so He knows the things of God better than we do; but the good news is that we now have power over him.

Recognize

The Choir's Anniversary

Everyone is so excited! New robes, visiting churches and choirs, guest speakers and lots of cute boys. Everyone has new hair styles, and beautiful church hats. As I recall a particular anniversary, it was the first time that the pastor's daughter got to sing her song. Everyone was making a big fuss over the pastor's daughter. She was only about 8 years old, but as God is my witness, her gift was not in the area of singing.

During this time of celebration, I don't think anyone was worshiping God or hearing from Him. Well, maybe that is an over-statement, but it just didn't seem spiritual at all; it was a show. The choir anniversary was a time for everyone to get his or her day in the limelight. If you were regularly a late comer, you had better make your way to the church earlier this day to get a seat. The choir anniversary, not the worship service, would always be standing room only.

It's time for the choir to march in. Everyone stands now as if to meet the king. All of the choir members look very lovely, even the once-a-year choir members. They march in with great pride and loud voices. They were not only looking good, but also sounding great. Their moves were better than the moves on Soul Train. My friends and I knew all the moves as we would watch them in rehearsals. We would stand over to the side keeping in sync with their every motion.

I liked imitating the choir director. She was always waving her arms and pointing while keeping in step with the others. She had the choir under her complete control with every gesture. And her robe was always the bomb! It was the

Recognize

same color as the choir's, but it was made totally different. It almost looked like an oversized outfit. The choir director always set the tone for the choir.

I would always look over at my grandmother. After all, she made all of the robes. She would say, "Don't the choir look great?" She would smile approvingly as if she were the mother of the bride. Then she would frown and say, "She got her nerve marching in the choir! She didn't ever pay me for that robe. She is gonna pay me for that robe." She would remain mad until the girl would make it up to the choir stand. Then she would still be talking under her breath. I would finally say "Ok, Ok, talk to her after the anniversary." But she would still be "in a funk" as others would march in who hadn't paid her yet.

The choir's anniversary was sheer excitement for me as a "shorty." It was almost like a battle of the voices. One choir would get up and sing a song, while the other choir would sit in judgment. The other choir would get up and try to outdo the previous choir, and so on and so on. If the choir director was "gay," we would give him extra points because he had some moves for you, along with attitude. The choir with the director who would lead a song, direct the choir with one hand, and play the organ with the other hand while standing would get the entire church off its feet.

The church would rock for hours non-stop. By the time the speaker would get up, the church would be half-empty. Most of the choirs would be gone, and the kids would be in the halls playing. People would be too tired to hear the Word, plus we all had school the next day. I could never remember what the preacher preached about on the choir anniversary.

The choir anniversary wasn't about God. It was about getting to see a free gospel concert, getting all dressed up, and having a lot of fun.

Attending church and not understanding the purpose for why you are there is a waste of time. Some people feel that going to church is enough, but what is important is your relationship with God. Isaiah 55:6-9 says; "Seek the Lord while He may be found. Call upon Him while He is near. Let the wicked forsake his way, and the unrighteous man his thoughts. Let him return to the Lord and He will have mercy on him and to our God. For He will abundantly pardon. For our thoughts are not His thoughts."

Recognize

The Holy Ghost #1

My Baptist church had regular shouters. Shouting is what folk do when the Spirit is high in the church. In some cases, good music would invoke the mood. Folk would dance or run around in what appeared to be a hypnotic state, and in some cases, move their feet in a fast rhythmic motion while waving their hands.

I kept a close eye on these shouters, because you never knew when you would get hit in the face with a flying purse. My attitude was, I didn't care how much you were in the Spirit, if you hit me with your purse you were going to get hit back! Once the music started, we knew that Sister Smith was going to take off running and shout until her wig would be sideways. I wasn't sure if I wanted that Holy Ghost. I didn't want anything that would make me look silly or make me lose my mind. Some people would shout so wild that it took all the Ushers to hold them down or worst yet, they would step on your foot with those pointed heels. I wasn't very nice to people who "caught" the ghost while sitting next to me. If they looked like they were about to do me some harm, I would push them into the aisle.

It was always funny to look up into the choir-stand. The choir was always "cuttin' up," particularly if the preacher was preaching really hard. For example, the preacher would say, "Can I get an AMEN?" and the choir would say "AMEN!" The preacher would say, "Can I get a witness?" and the choir would wave their hands. The preacher would say, "Ain't He all right?" while pointing up to heaven, and the choir would say, "YES! He's all right". By this time the organ player has

Recognize

fallen in sync with the choir's every word. When the choir would say AMEN, the organ player would hit a chord. When the choir said, "He's all right", the organ player would hit a chord, and when the choir waved their hands, the organ player would hit a few more chords. There was a certain unscripted rhythm here as if orchestrated by the Spirit.

When the preacher would "get to doing the holy dance," the entire choir would shout, dance, kick, and run. After about 10 minutes, the choir would look a complete mess from where I was sitting. Some would still be bucking, and others fanning themselves or someone else. Yet some would still be waving their arms as if they were trying to land a huge plane. Don't get me wrong, I didn't think it was all just for show. I really believe that God showed up every now and then. I also believed that some members were really living the good life, and were sold out for God. It was just hard to recognize the difference.

I had a few friends who would catch the Holy Ghost. I would ask them what did it feel like and how do I get it. I felt that God had His favorite picks and they all were the people that shouted. The only confusing part was that many of these people were mean and insensitive. After they were done shouting, they were back to no good. I never could get a clear answer on how to catch the Holy Ghost. I was always made to feel that the only reason I didn't shout in church was because I wasn't good enough. I decided that one day I would be so good, I would read my Bible all the time, and I would act right in church to the point that God would let me catch the real Holy Ghost.

Even though many of these churchgoers were "saved",

they needed to be delivered from many of the demons that were riding their backs. If you don't recognize that you have a demon, you won't know how "to pray it up off you."

Now just what is a demon? My associations with learned scholars in my later years always dismiss this concept as a superstition or language passed on from an ancient culture. To hold on to the idea of a demon is mystical, dark and incomprehensible to many "more sophisticated Christians." They go to the psychologists and psychiatrists and spend much time and money on medication. They also go to therapy for their neurotic and bi-polar disorders. The sister in church, however, not able to afford such "high priced exorcism," releases her "primal scream" at church and returns home, justified and cured.

Likewise, what is the real Holy Ghost? I say the "real" Holy Ghost, because I knew that there was also a fake 'ghost', and there wasn't anything holy about it. There was this lady who had a very street look about her. She would wear nice looking clothes, but they never looked clean. She wore a hat that had feathers all around it with a few sticking straight up. She had red eyes like Mary at the liquor store. She walked like a man and she never smiled.

I would always watch her and she would always shout at the same time during the service. After she was done shouting, she would look over at me and stick her tongue out and whip her head back around toward the front of the church. She looked like a witch, and she may well have been whatever the official term is for people engaged in this ungodly craft. I would always stare in her direction, and when she looked over at me, I would frown at her and put my

Recognize

two index fingers together to make a cross and put them in front of my face so she could see the cross.

One day she was up shouting, and I asked my grandmother was that the Holy Ghost we were looking at. She told me to shut up and pay attention to the Word. I really wanted to know, so I asked her, "Who is that lady?" My grandmother said she was somebody's auntie from in the church. "Where did she come from?" My grandmother was getting really irritated with me and asked me, "Why are you asking so many questions about that lady?" I told her that the lady reminded me of a crazy lady I used to see at my dad's liquor store. "That lady ain't crazy," my grandmother said. She told me to stop judging people. I said, "Okay, but grandma, I want you to see something. As soon as that lady sits down," I told her, "watch her stick her tongue out at me." My grandmother paid me no attention.

As soon as that lady sat down, I stared over at her for about 3 minutes. Then it happened! She looked over at me as if she knew I was looking at her, and she stuck her tongue out at me. "Grandma, did you see that?" I asked. "No!" She said, "now sit here and pay attention."

It was something about her spirit I didn't like. There was something about the orchestration of the shout which reminded me of the sort of expression which was opposite of the spirit of church rhythm. I really can't say more about it, but what I have learned in my later life about discernment was present here. She "read me" and I "read her." She "recognized" my sprit and I "recognized" hers. It was something about mine she didn't like, and it was something about hers that I didn't like. Sometimes, I would stare at her and plead the "Blood of Jesus" under my breath. And, almost as if she could hear me, she would look in my direction, frown, stick out her tongue and move her seat. I knew I wasn't all that holy, but I truly desired the Spirit of God. She, on the other hand, was straight up "off the hook evil!" She would shout so wild at church so that when the Usher tried to sit her down, she would come out of her "make believe" trance and tell them to take their hands off her as nasty as she could. In my opinion, she wasn't there to serve the Lord. She was there for some other reason; maybe to disrupt the service.

I wanted to know more about the Holy Ghost. I would ask my grandmother lots of questions. "How do you know if you got the real thing?" I would ask my grandmother, and she would say; "only God really knows." "He knows your heart," she said. "He knows your life style. Also, it's not for us to judge others. Just worry about yourself. You'll catch the Holy Ghost one day."

I could tell that there were two different kinds of spirits at work even then. One made you look foolish, and didn't seem to change you. The other seemed painless and peaceful. It seemed to give a sense of peace, wisdom and beauty accompanied by a tear—and a feeling of being all choked up with joy. For some reason I could see a difference, and I didn't want to catch the wrong ghost. I prayed daily that God would keep me from all evil, and that when it was my turn to catch the Holy Ghost, please make it be the good one.

I had an encyclopedia of Bible stories. I kept my head in these books. There wasn't a story in the Bible that I didn't

Recognize

know. My favorite story was about Joseph and his multi-colored coat. My best friend Barbara and I would challenge each other on who could tell the story the best.

Unclean spirits are everywhere even in the church, but don't use this as a reason not to attend. There is also healing in the church. Think of it this way, when you go to the hospital there are sick people there, but there are also doctors and nurses there who can help make you better. Satan was over the choir in heaven and he still thinks that he is in charge now. This is why we have so much turmoil in many of our choirs today. There is also the spirit of vanity in the churches. Everyone wants to be the Queen. It's a spirit of looking good for others and not looking or doing your best for God. I am reminded of how David played his instrument so well for King Saul that the unclean spirits left him. If our choirs would sing to the glory of God and not as if they were trying to compete in some local talent show, we would have more people delivered (it is God's anointing that will destroy the yoke of bondage).

A PRAYER
FOR CHURCH - GOERS
AND LEADERS

Father God, I pray that we Your people would take our eyes off of others and place them on You. I pray that the talent that You have given me will be used for Your glory. Lord, instruct me on what it is that You would have me to do. Lord, I am a church going sinner and I need Your help and Your spirit. I also need Your Apostles, Prophets, Preachers, Teachers, and Evangelists, and they need me too as I am a part of the body. You are my deliverer and comforter. Father, help me to be what You have designed me to be in Your kingdom. I pray that as I work/volunteer, and attend church that I will walk in love and meet in Your house to receive Your Word, and to share Your love. Teach me, O Lord, how to look past my faults and the faults of others. Please Lord, help me to look past my tears and grief and be able to receive and give Your abundant love. Lord, I attend church and we need _____from You. Please hear my prayer, in Jesus name I pray. AMEN!

Recognize

Meet Timothy

Finally, I am old enough to get a summer job. The line was long at the youth center and there were only so many jobs to go around. Timothy was reviewing all of the applications, and making sure that the applicants were old enough to work by checking our birth certificates. You had to show proof that you were at least 13 years or older. Once he verified your age, he would ask you a few simple questions. Why do you want to work at this center? Do you have any skills or talents that would enhance the center?

I was a little nervous because I didn't know if I would measure up. Many of the girls and boys were a little older and looked very athletic. I didn't know what to expect. Many of the people standing in line had on shorts and gym shoes, but my mom told me to put on one of my school outfits so I could look nice.

She really needed me to get this job. She no longer had my dad's income; he was living with one of his "hoes" as my mom put it. I looked nice, but I didn't look athletic at all.

As I got closer to the handsome man asking the questions, I was now in hearing distance. I was able to hear what type of questions Timothy was asking each applicant. Some of the positions available were: Classroom teacher for three different age groups, activity workers, activity supervisors, event coordinators and ball players.

Most of the people were interested in the ball playing positions. They were actually paying young people to play ball just to keep them off the streets and out of gangs. I decided to go for the event coordinator position. I didn't even consider going for any of the athletic positions. I didn't want to consent to an early death. Some of those girl ball-players were like giants and had muscles larger than my brothers. I didn't know girls could grow so large. I didn't play any type of ball. I didn't like any type of sport, and wasn't interested in playing any sports. I was just hoping that the youth center had something that I could do. "Why do you want to work here?"

Timothy asked. Answering without appearing nervous, I said, "Because I'd like to help my mom pay some of the bills. She's a single mother of seven, and I feel that I am old enough to help out."

He didn't give me any indication if my answer was acceptable or not. He just jumped right to the next question. "What skills do you bring to the table?" "I help my mom with my four little sisters, so that would make me a great supervisor. I also worked in my aunt's store on weekends (I purposely left off the word liquor) as a cashier. I helped her restock and keep inventory, so I am great at coordinating things. I can also dance a little and can teach the girls at this center how to dance."

"What position are you applying for? Can you play any type of sports?" I began to stutter. "I-I-I like sports, and I can learn to play. I-I-I-I have brothers who can teach me sports. I even like the outfits that sports people wear. If I need to learn sports, I-I-I-I-I can go to the library and read about sports. I even watch sports on TV in my spare time." By this time my mind had left my body. I knew I was rambling, but I couldn't stop myself. I just knew he was going to tell me to go home and come back next year. I started to feel sick. I just knew I sounded like an idiot. The last thing I said about even watching sports on TV was so stupid. So Timothy looked at me with a smirk on his face and said, "How would you like to be my sports coordinator?" I said yes, yes, yes! I was so happy! I wanted to kiss his feet. He told me to report to work on Monday sharply at 8a.m. This was the start of my first summer job. I worked for Timothy for four years and he taught me many lessons that I carry with me today.

Life at the youth center was eventful and challenging. People were always getting shot and the youth center was always the meeting place for gang fights.

Timothy was a wise militant kind of guy. He always had on his red, black, and green crochet beanie hat, and his black power fist necklace. He was always teaching me about my blackness. He told me that the only true power was to get a good education. All that church stuff I always talked about was just another way for the white man to brainwash our people. Praying to some make believe God was foolish and a waste of time. He would always say that the power was within me. You are the one who can make things happen, not some make believe God. I told him that I knew God was real and that no one could make me believe differently.

I couldn't understand why Timothy was always talking about the black man and the white man. I used to watch all of the "I Have a Dream" speeches, civil rights marches, and documentaries on Martin Luther King, Jr. I watched other black leaders during black history month, but I hadn't experienced any white person hating me for the color of my

61

Recognize

skin. Granted, I didn't know very many whites, only my school teachers and they seemed very nice.

I remember one day it was raining outside, so the entire summer camp had to stay indoors. We would always have a rap session on rainy days. We would discuss things from teenage pregnancy to how to be successful as a black man or woman. Timothy would teach that the white man was always keeping the black man down. He was always saying that we are still waiting for our "40 acres and a mule." His comments would remind me of how Pharaoh kept the children of Israel down. But because God showed favor to the children of Israel, they eventually became victorious.

I couldn't buy into Timothy's militant attitude, so I would never really participate in any of the conversations. I liked and respected him, and I didn't want to openly speak against him. I felt that Timothy would have been an even more effective, awesome person if he had taken his educational knowledge and coupled it with the knowledge of God. I could look into his eyes and see "deep hurt." And I believe that hurt (where ever it came from) caused him to not believe in God.

Timothy believed that the power was within you and not in some make believe invisible God. And I, on the other hand, believed that you have all power through God. It was hard for me to prove it because my life was so messed up, but I knew that God was still able even if it seemed like He wasn't showing up in my life.

One rainy day, Timothy had me to get one of the rooms prepared for a youth discussion. I didn't have anything to do, so he asked me to sit in. They were discussing the roles between a man and a woman. Keep in mind this discussion was taking place between 13-18 year old adolescents. Most of the time the young people were talking over one another and Timothy had to be the referee. One of the young men who obviously had a crush on me said, "So Ms. Toni, what do you think about a woman servicing her man?" A hush came over the room. I had never participated in these discussions before mainly because I didn't want Timothy to know that I didn't share his opinion on a lot of things. My viewpoint was mainly from a biblical perspective. I also had a lot of respect and love for Timothy. He gave me my first job. He understood my home situation, and he was always trying to teach me some life lessons. But since Timothy didn't ask the question, I felt that it was my time to say what I had to say.

As I tried to gather my thoughts, all of a sudden I couldn't put what I wanted to say into words. I know there is a spot in the bible that talks about a virtuous woman, but I knew that the youth at the center weren't trying to hear that. My mind began to race with how Cinderella would answer this question or what would my mother say. This was a time where it was better to be hard like nothing bothers you, than to act like a little, soft girl. You got more respect on the Westside if you were brave and had an attitude. I put my hands on my hips and started rolling my neck and said, "You better get that Henry the Eighth mess up out of here! Women don't serve men anymore. Men don't deserve to be served. If anything, men need to be serving women." I was basing my answer off of what I saw in my own house. My mother would cook dinner, have my father's plate ready, and he would never show up. I said, "I will never serve a man, that's OUT!" All the girls began to cheer me on, and I felt

Recognize

like I had just won a round in a wrestling match.

Timothy's eyebrows went up, and the girls were still screaming and slapping five to one another. I got big points from the girl's club. Not because my answer was so great, but because I had much attitude. The young man that asked the question had a comeback, however. He said, "I bet if I put this on you (grabbing his genital area like he was Michael Jackson) you would serve me." I said, "You have to find it first."

Everyone began to laugh. By this time the conversation was a little out of control and Timothy put an end to the discussion. I felt energized coming up with comments that would hurt his manhood, and I didn't know why. He didn't do anything to me. Not recognizing that the devil was setting me up for the "spirit of Jezebel" to influence my life.

Later on that evening, back in Timothy's office, Timothy said, "You were pretty talkative today. Where did all that negative energy come from?" "It wasn't from the heart," I said, "I was just trying to get the crowd going." Timothy said, "Well you are a pretty good actress, but I really don't think it was all acting. You need to know that you are who you are not because of your father or mother, but because of what's in here (he pointed to his chest)."

He was talking to me as if he knew my thoughts, as if he knew my feelings, as if he knew that I was just tripping because my dad had left. I was impressed that he was so in tune. I said to myself that Timothy would make a great preacher if he only knew God. I listened, but I wasn't trying to hear any of his logic because much of it wasn't based on the things of God.

I knew that I had strength even as a young girl. I could also hear my grandmother saying, "It's the woman's seed whose heel will bruise the head of Satan." In the garden of Eden, Satan made us weak, but God has made us strong. We need to recognize this fact, and use it for the glory of God and to destroy the work of the devil and not each other.

Recognize

A PRAYER FOR THE MAN

Dear Lord, I know that all power is in Your hands, and I pray right now that You would heal my heart and touch me with Your hand of love. Help me to forgive my mother for hurting me, my father for hurting me, and for every female that has hurt and belittled me. Lord, please give me back my strength. Father, help me to use my gifts and restore everything that Satan has stolen from me. Teach me how to build, protect, communicate, grow-in-love, and be what You've designed me to be. Give me more love for woman, and more love for myself. Father, with You I can do all things. I believe by faith that You are with me, and as I pray and listen to Your voice I will be a better person in the earth and in the body of Christ. Thank You, Lord, for hearing my prayer. AMEN!

Meet Barbara

I met Barbara at the age of 12 going on 13. She and I had a lot in common. She had four sisters and I had four sisters. The only difference was that I had two older brothers and she had none. And all of my sisters were younger than me, but Barbara had two older sisters. Being the oldest girl gave me a "bossy" side, people would say. I'd like to refer to it as my leadership and protective characteristics. Barbara was born in June and so was I. She liked going to church and so did I. We both loved telling bible stories. Barbara knew the bible well and was able to teach me a few things. Her mother was very active in the church and Barbara and her sister had to attend church in the same way my sisters and I experienced.

We always were together and people thought she and I were sisters. We often dressed alike and enjoyed just sitting on her porch "tripping" with the other kids. After our eighth grade graduation, we were planning to attend the same high school. We were going to pull every string that needed to be pulled to ensure we would be at the same high school. My mother wanted me at the same high school as my brothers. Barbara's mom wanted her at the same high school as her sisters. But as fate would have it, we ended up going to the same high school.

High school itself was a lot of fun. The only difficult times were when we would run into girls from girl gangs while going back and forth to school. Neither Barbara nor I were in a gang, and never had on gang colors when approached. Certain colors would get you an instant "butt whippin'." I

Recognize

would always tell Barbara to look normal and maybe those girls up ahead will just walk past us. It was always too many of them for Barbara, my blade, and I to handle.

"So, who you represent?" someone would always ask us. We would always say that we represented Jesus and they wouldn't do anything other than check our pockets for anything of value, and then take our lunch money. I was quick to fight more so than Barbara, but I wouldn't dare try to take on more than two girls at a time, even with my blade. Some of those girls looked like they had just gotten out of prison. The only way you knew that they were girls is that they had breasts. I always carried a blade, but in my heart I didn't want to use it. I was told that you could go to jail if you stabbed someone, even in self-defense.

One thing Barbara and I would do for fun was play church. She was the preacher and I directed the choir and was in her AMEN corner. Barbara was really good at imitating the preacher and we both were good at "play shouting." I remember her mother telling us both that one day the Spirit of the Lord was going to get a hold of us and our days for playing church would be over. Barbara's mother was very religious, and was on the nurse's board at a nearby church. She had a lot of health challenges and died 5 years later, only in her early thirties.

Barbara and I remained friends for years, and we experienced a lot together. I was more of a fighter than Barbara, and I would always protect her from other girls "jumping on her." If they wanted to fight Barbara, they had to deal with me. I didn't mind pulling out my blade, but I was always hoping that I would never have to use it.

As we got older, Barbara would sometimes date guys that would like to hit and/or toss her around too often. I didn't know if it was because she didn't have any brothers or what. I would always threaten her boyfriends to leave her alone or deal with my brothers, cousins or worse yet, some of the rough guys from the liquor store. All I had to do was get my father to give them a few bucks and they would burn down half of Chicago for me. My mother always told me that I was always putting my nose in other people's business, but I didn't appreciate a man putting their hands on a lady. I didn't have any respect for any man who felt big "boxing on a woman." My opinion was, if you want to feel like a man, fight somebody your own size. Fight another man.

I had a few dates that would try to strong-arm me and take sex without my consent. I taught them to back off once I pulled out my blade. I wasn't shy at all about pulling out my blade. I remember guys having their way with the women at the liquor store and in other places. I remembered my mother was able to get my dad off of her one day, when he came in drunk she put a knife through his chest. I hated seeing my dad lay in all that blood, but my mother had taken her share of beatings over the years. I just knew that there was some unknown spirit that was let loose which caused people to act crazy. My prayer was that I would learn to recognize it. I would just pray to God at night that this malevolent spirit didn't ever get the best of me. I really never wanted some man hitting, controlling, or trying to rape me.

My grandmother always had words of wisdom for me. She would provide me with the following wisdom: "You have to make the best out of life. Nothing in life is free, and you have to fight for what you want. It's a mean world out here,

Recognize

so spending time crying over spilled milk is a waste of energy. Prayer fixes everything. If you don't stand for something, you'll fall for anything, and remember no matter how tough things get, there is always someone worse off than you."

Sometimes I would tell Barbara to pray until things got better. I just think she really missed her mom. We need our mothers at every stage in life, but to lose your mother early has to be hard. I think her hurt caused her to begin hanging out with the wrong crowd. She started getting "high", and began to drink too much. I would be so mad at her when she called herself doing drugs. She didn't even look right getting high. Her spirit belonged to God and I was convinced that all she needed to do was pray. I didn't like seeing her that way and I didn't like her new friends, so we started spending less time with each other. Although her faith in God had seemed to be fading, God's love for her didn't fade. All I could think about was the time that the women in the liquor store told me that liquor helped take the pain away. So could it be that pain ushers in other spirits? If so, beware of hurts, and things that cause pain. Take your hurts and pain to the Lord in prayer before you become bewitched. The spirit of depression was trying to take Barbara over, which is one of the bewitching spirits, but God's care was the ultimate victor. I didn't know many warfare prayers at the time, but I have learned some since then. Since it wasn't cool to be depressed, many people in her condition were taught to drink their pain away.

It was better to be drunk than depressed. That was Westside. That was what the grown people did. Society made it very easy for us to drink our pain away. Liquor stores on every corner were the economy. It brought in money to the stores and demons to the households.

Although Barbara had gotten off track, her habit and discipline of going to church helped her get rid of her demons. She is now an evangelist preaching the Word of God with conviction and fire. When I go hear her speak, I can sometimes see that little girl who used to play church on the back porch.

Trauma, disappointment, sickness/disease, and other misfortunes can open a corridor for Satan and other unclean spirits to cohabitate with you. Drinking and other addictions may look like acceptable medicine when you are dealing with pain, but Jesus asked in Luke 6:39 can the blind lead the blind? Will they not both fall into a ditch? In the same chapter around the 43rd verse it talks about a tree being known by its fruit. As my grandmother would always say, there is always someone worse off than you. So, with that said, I encourage you to continue to sow good seeds in your life and just know by faith that harvest time is just a season away.

Recognize

A PRAYER FOR ANYONE WHO FEELS TRAUMATIZED

Lord, I pray the 91st Psalm over everyone reading and confessing this prayer. Lord, thank You for being my secret place, and for being my refuge and my fortress. Lord, I thank You for being all of the spiritual medicine that I need. I thank You for being the King of Glory in my life. In Psalm 24 starting at the 7th verse, You tell me to lift up my head. Lord, I pray that You would turn my mourning into joy. I pray that You would restore me, guide me, and protect me from all hurt, harm and danger. Keep me in Your perfect peace as my mind stays on You Lord. Cover me with Your Son's precious blood, in Jesus name I pray, AMEN

1st Year in High School-- Time to meet Derrick

I really looked forward to high school. I was told that the juniors and seniors would make fun of me by calling me names like "fresh meat". I was already mentally prepared for the abuse. Initially I adjusted. So far so good. I was really enjoying high school. The boys were cute, the teachers were cool, and the people were somewhat friendly. Then it happened.

One day I was walking to the gym to try out for the pom-pom squad. All of the kids were walking along the walls and were under the complete control of one boy that looked like he was Satan's son. He was shiny black and very muscular with very thick eyebrows. He looked like he should have been in college. He was larger than any of the other boys at school, not in weight, but in muscular size. It was almost as if he had done time in prison. As I walked down the center of the hall, people were looking at me as if I had just signed my own death wish. As I looked up, I was standing face to face with what I was guessing was a boy. He looked at me as if he was trying to disintegrate me with his eyes. I looked at him as if to say get out of the way fool.

I moved to the right, he moved to the right, I moved to the left and he moved to the left. I asked him to get out of the way, and he actually bit me on my back and took off running. The people on the walls were just looking as if they were shocked that he didn't do much more to me. I examined my upper shoulder to see how much damage was done and then I went to the nurse's station and she patched me up.

Recognize

The next day, I felt this excruciating pain in my back. As I turned around I could see someone running through the crowd. It was, indeed, him! And he did it again! He bit me! I went to the nurse's station again and explained to the nurse that there is a boy at this school that was making a meal out of me.

The security guard wanted me to point him out. I pointed to the boy that looked like and felt like a madman-- he was crazy. The guard said that's Derrick. We get complaints about him all the time. He likes to beat up people, but I never heard of him biting anyone. Just stay away from him. "That's all, stay away from him." I said. "What about him staying away from me?" It appeared that everyone was taking this situation very lightly, but I couldn't let this stop me from trying out for pom-pom. In my heart I knew that I would be an asset to the pom-pom team. I could dance. I was in pretty good shape, and I had a lot of ideas for new dance routines.

Before the actual tryouts, (a white woman who had no dancing skills, a gym teacher) Ms. Misencik and Ms. Brown (who was the girl's basketball coach) laid out the rules for the tryouts. They were both apart of the tryout panel along with about five upper classmen. All we had to do in order to make the team was dance to the music and repeat the routine that was just demonstrated 10 minutes ago. We had to smile, state why we wanted to be a pom-pom girl, and for extra points we could show some type of athletic ability. I was going for the extra points. After all, hanging out at the "Y" with all those athletes I developed some athletic abilities.

I could see all the boys on the outside of the door trying

to see who was trying to represent the school. Derrick was even out there pushing the other kids out the way so that he could get a front view of the tryouts. It was now my turn.

The music started. I nailed the routine. Dancing was one of the only things I felt confident about. When I hear music, I feel God. I believe that music was created by God, and hearing the sound of the piano, trumpets, drums, etc., gave me a lot of energy. In addition, I had seen about 11 other girls tryout before me and I could mark their mistakes. They didn't even attempt the extra credit piece. After my routine, I displayed my athletic abilities, and smiling was something that I did naturally. I couldn't wait to be a part of the team. I needed to belong to something and this was a sure win.

People were cheering for me, even the new girls who were trying out as well. Derrick was outside jumping up and down. He then opened the door and said, "You Got It Girl". I was so embarrassed. Both gym teachers looked pleased, but I couldn't read the other panelists as they had their heads down. I guess they were adding up all of my wonderful scores.

Tryouts were over. We were told that names would be posted outside the next morning. Barbara tried out too. We went to the girl's locker room, showered, dressed and walked home. "Girl, you got down." Barbara said. I told Barbara that she had a few moves herself. Barbara said "I know you made it. I just hope I did too." "Girl don't worry, you made it." I said.

When the morning came, I couldn't wait to see my name on the board. I dreamed all night of how I was going to share new routines with the girls. I had plans to let them know that I already knew about dance competitions from being at the

Recognize

YMCA; we could put this pom-pom team on the map, as they had never, ever won a pom-pom competition. I was ready to be all that I could be, and I couldn't wait to get to school. There were so many people standing in front of the list that I couldn't see anything, so I waited my turn.

Some people were walking past me and giving me an off look which made me want to see the list even the more. Maybe they were jealous that I made it and they had not. When I finally got close enough to view the list, I ran my fingers up and down the list twice, now three times, but I didn't see my name! My name was not on the list. I didn't panic. I knew it had to be some kind of mistake. Barbara's name wasn't on the list either, but she wasn't tripping like I was. I had run my finger up and down the list for maybe about the tenth time and the list had not changed. My name was not on the list.

I went to both gym teachers to see what the problem was. While I was trying to get a logical explanation, I was told that it's not up to them, but the upper classmen. They are the ones who make the final decision. I was so very disappointed. I couldn't understand why I wasn't picked. I needed to know if I had done something wrong. I needed to know if I could tryout again. I needed some answers.

As I was switching classes later on in the day, I saw one of the pom-pom panelists and some of her friends. I asked her if I could talk to her. "Sure." she said. We walked about 10 paces and I asked her why I didn't make the team. All she had to say was "maybe next year", and walked away. As she got back with her friends, they all looked in my direction and shared in a good laugh.

I didn't have the heart to tell Timothy that I didn't make the team. He had begun to think so much of me and my talent. I started staying after school and watching the pom-pom girls rehearse. Now it was my turn to laugh! They needed a lot of help and their only helper was Ms. Misencik. She would say, "Shake it like this, shake it like that." I would look up from doing my homework and would always get a good laugh. Ms. Misencik looked like a big-butt, short pumpkin fighting off killer bumblebees from the way she was swinging those pom-poms. I would get tickled every time she would try to show them a move.

The day after tryouts, there was a note on my locker that read, "You should have made the team." The word should was spelled (Chod). I knew it was Derrick. I just snatched it down and was hoping he wasn't anywhere near by. That biting was getting on my nerves.

One day I was heading to the auditorium for a school program, and spotted Derrick. I felt safe because teachers and students surrounded me. I kept my eyes on him just to insure he didn't get any ideas. As I continued to look in his direction, he spotted me. I could tell that he was going to try something right in the open in front of everyone. I could feel it in my spirit. I told one teacher that Derrick was in the auditorium and I believed that he was going to attack me. She told me to relax, that I was safe. Next, I told one of the security guards the same thing. He told me that everything was under control. I felt led to keep my eyes on Derrick for a while longer, and all of a sudden he started toward me like a pit bull after a piece of steak. He jumped over chairs, knocked some students down and pushed others out of his way. I took off yelling, "Help, help, help! He's

Recognize

going to get me! HELP!!!" He caught me, tackled me and took a big plug out of my leg. I had to go to a nearby hospital to get a shot, ointment, and gauze. Needless to say, this situation was getting out of control, and no one could protect me from Derrick. It was as if everyone was afraid of him, and acted as if his behavior was normal. I on the other hand, felt like I had died and was living in the twilight zone.

The school hired a specialist to come in to interview Derrick and to analyze his behavior. In the meantime, there was an order of protection issued to keep him away from me. The following few weeks were quiet. I think the counseling and the order of protection worked, for a while. Guys were not afraid to speak to me any longer. I think they were under the impression that if they tried to talk to me they would have to deal with Derrick and his team of internal demons. They may have been correct.

One day, someone broke into my locker and took mostly candy and suckers. Derrick terrorized the entire school for weeks. Anyone walking around with gum or candy would get jumped on. Derrick was on a mission to find out who broke into my locker. On the flip side of things, one day I was sitting on my mother's back porch with a male friend drinking some kool-aid because it was too hot to sit out front. All of a sudden, I was hit in the face with a brick. Derrick threw a brick at me and bruised my forehead. I had to be rushed to a nearby hospital and have my head stitched up. My mom and I went to the school to report the incident and a complaint was filed. I was becoming a regular at the hospital with bites, cuts, busted heads, etc. I couldn't understand why I was under so much attack.

"Toni to the office please, Toni to the office." This is what I could hear over the loud speaker at school. I was being asked to speak with Derrick's "shrink." "Why do I have to speak with her?" I asked. "Well, she believes that you can help Derrick with his dysfunctional behavior," the office clerk said. As I sat down, I was in the room with a "shrink" who looked more like a witch doctor. She was white with yellow teeth and gray hair, a young face but old looking hands. The nurse was in the room and a family counselor representative. I felt like I was on trial.

The questions began. "Where were you and what were you doing when Derrick first bit you? And the second time? Have you ever stood up to him? What about coming on to him?" The questions were endless. "I have a report of when he busted your forehead," the shrink said, "and after speaking with him he stated that he was not trying to hurt you. That he was trying to hit someone else. Were you with someone when you got hit in the head with the brick?" "Yes," I said. "I was with a boy from my neighborhood." What were you doing? "Nothing, just sitting on the porch drinking kool-aid," I said. "I think this made Derrick jealous and that's why he threw the brick and you got hurt instead of the boy." "Either way, he's crazy," I said.

The shrink continued, "Well Toni, I think Derrick has a crush on you. (Brilliant! I said to myself. I'm an unemployed high school freshman, and I could have told you that). He has been in and out of shelters and he has been beaten as a child," she continued. "Biting you is his way of showing his affection for you. We are going to try something new with Derrick and we would like for you to assist us with this." "WHAT? Why do I have to be apart of a crazy person's

Recognize

rehab? Haven't I suffered enough?" I was having this conversation with my inner self, but on the outside I just nodded in agreement.

I was not aware that Derrick may have had childhood problems, but he was also being used by Satan. I was under demonic attack and Derrick was being used as Satan's agent. Derrick was an easy prey for Satan because he was under the impression that pain equaled love. When you are taught at an early age when life is innocent, and love is expected, it's easy to think that all the mistreatment you received as a child must be what love is. This is a trick of the devil and he puts his assignment out on folk at an early age.

This kind of diagnosis was my first introduction to psychology and religion. The view that neurosis parallels what I have learned to "recognize" as demons was first introduced here. This malfunction comes from a trauma experienced earlier which is inconsistent with the victim's view of himself. The trauma causes repression, but since the pain cannot be totally repressed, it shows itself in bodily effects. Sometimes in sleep disorder, skin disorder or simply inappropriate behavior. His therapist told me that they were training him to express himself in a more non-violent way and that I should see a change in his behavior. I felt—and still feel—that what Derrick needed is what all people "under attack" need—deliverance! Prayer, love and the recognition of what is operating within their mind and body. Many psychologists who may not be familiar with "God language" call these disorders neurosis and psychosis—I call it what Jesus calls it—Demons.

Derrick started giving me flowers (dandelions) by sticking his head in my classrooms and throwing them in my direction and running off. Many of the kids found these events funny, but they did not laugh for fear of getting a busted lip from Derrick. I still had to keep my eye on Derrick because he would sometimes throw candy at me, and if I wasn't looking I could get hit in the face with some Now and Laters or some jaw breakers. He was very strong and had a good aim, so I needed to be ready at all times to catch his new gesture of love.

Derrick's lack of love as a child caused him to behave in many ungodly ways. He was abused as a child and had associated pain with love. He too suffered from early abandonment, abuse, anger, rejection, and many disappointments of not getting a real family but being moved around from one foster parent to another. These were common threads in my community. They would always send family counselors to the school to deal with the crazy acting kids, but what they needed was a deliverance service right dab in the middle of the school. Now that prayer is taken out of the school we see even more demonic activities. More date rape, shootings, and students fighting the teachers. I'm sure the witches are happy.

Recognize

A PRAYER FOR ALL
FOSTER CHILDREN

Father God, I am Your child whether I'm with a foster parent, a grandparent, or even if I have no parents at all. It is You Lord who've made me, and I accept You as my everything. I pray for Your loving protection over my life. Teach me Your ways and not the ways of ungodly people. Order my footsteps and cover me with people who will love me. Send Your ministering angels to look after me, and teach me how to wear Your full armor found in Ephesians 6:13 so that I would be able to stand in the evil days. Lord change everything about me that is not like You. Make me a new creation in You Lord, and show me my value, IN JESUS NAME, AMEN!

Meet what I call "White Walls"

A "White Wall" experience is simple: it's where all the walls were white. Walls in hospitals are white. You have white walls in most dental offices, and many apartment buildings have white painted walls. I have had many interesting experiences behind the "White Walls."

Since I didn't make the pom-pom team I went out for track and field. I was pretty good at distance running and thought this would be a good second choice. I made the team, but wasn't having any fun. It was just a bunch of working out and running around until you drop. The only bonus was that the boys were all cute.

One day we stayed inside the gym instead of running outside because the weather was bad. As I ran, for what appeared to be about 50 laps, I could hear the track coach yelling "Who is that running flat footed? Who is that running flat footed? Pick up your feet!!!!" It was me. If I ran any other way my feet would hurt. I figured if I just kept on running, he'd never know it was me as there had to be over 20 other kids in the gym.

The coach came along-side of me and ran with me for about 2 minutes and said "Pick up your feet!" As I picked up my feet, I got a really sharp pain in my right foot and fell to the ground. The coach and a few other concerned people ran over to assist me. My arch had dropped and my coach said it was serious. He took me home to my mother and she had to take me to a foot doctor.

Recognize

My mother was not happy! This entire incident made me feel like I made a stupid mistake trying out and making the track and field team.

The foot doctor told me that I had flat feet and that I needed to have surgery on both feet in order to stop the pain in my feet while running. My mom and I were on the same page for a change. We both thought that I just wouldn't run. On the other hand, in my neighborhood being able to run was an asset. As the doctor continued, he said, "She will either have the surgery now while she is still young, or later when she's older." He added that the cost of surgery would probably double and that I would be in more pain as I got older. Needless to say, I ended up in surgery and in the hospital for about three weeks.

The first time my feet hit the floor, I fell to the ground. The pain was too great. I was told that I would have to learn how to walk all over again. Every morning two physical therapists would come for me, pick me up, one on one arm and the other on the other arm. I would hold my feet up in the air so that they wouldn't touch the floor. They would say with a loud voice "Toni, you have to walk before we can release you". I couldn't, it would hurt too bad. I could only stand by shifting my weight from one foot to the other. I couldn't put one foot in front of the other. All they were trying to do was to get me to put one foot in front of the other. This appeared to be an impossible task.

A week after my surgery, a little black girl moved into my room with me. One thing that really stood out about her was that her hair was really, really nappy and hadn't been combed in days. She was about five or six, and I wanted to comb her hair and put it in some pretty braids the moment I saw her. What was so surprising about this little girl was that she could speak perfect English. She had excellent grammar and could read better than me. I was wondering if she was some type of little genius or something. Maybe her mom was a schoolteacher, but either way, she was a very interesting little person. She needed to have the same surgery, but only on one foot. I still felt sorry for her because the surgery was so painful that I wouldn't wish it on my worst enemy.

I heard her little voice after the nurses left our room, "What is your name?" she asked, "Toni, and yours?" "Sarah". "Hi Sarah, are you lonely over there?" I asked. "Yes, could you read me a story?" she asked. "Sure." I said. I figured I could get through the Cat and the Hat. "I can't walk, so you need to come over here." She got in my bed with her book and put the book in my lap. It was some type of adventure storybook with words that I had never seen before. All of a sudden I didn't feel like reading. "I have a better idea, why don't I braid your hair and make you look like a little princess." I said. "That would be great!" she said. "I've never had my hair braided before. My new mom and dad can't braid hair." I didn't catch the "NEW" part until her parents came to visit Sarah. They both were white.

Sarah had just been adopted and her "new" parents were making a big fuss over her. They really liked her hair and wanted to know if I could teach them how to do it. I wasn't sure if I could or not. It was something I was gifted with.

Sarah and I didn't talk much after her surgery, she had her new family there all the time and I didn't want to take away from all of the attention she was getting. She needed

Recognize

it. They treated her like a baby doll. They would carry her to the restroom, feed her, and constantly asked her if she was all right or if she needed anything. Much of the time she was getting a lot of that attention to the point that I wanted to yell out, "Yes, I need something, but I can't get up to get it. Hello, can somebody ask me if I'm OK?" Instead, I just kept my curtain drawn and eavesdropped on what was happening on the other side of it.

One day, Sarah asked me if I was sad. "Why?" I asked. She said, "I remember when I was in a shelter and no one would ever visit me, I was always sad. I see that no one ever visits you, so you must be sad." I guess I was sad. I just didn't notice because it was such a familiar feeling.

Walking was so painful and I was wondering what my feet looked like under those bandages. It was time for the stitches to come out as they were removing the bandages. My feet were swollen and purple. I had monster feet! I hated the doctor for what he had done to me. My mother said to him, "Did you have to put such big cuts on her feet? You doctors are all the same. Always cutting on folk just to get a buck or two!" The doctor said "It just looks worse than it is, once her feet heal, it won't look so bad." Now I was really sad. All I could think about was if I'd ever be able to wear sandals for the rest of my life.

The good news was I could go home in the morning. Well I guess it was good news. The doctor came in my room and said "Get ready to go home!" He said it with such enthusiasm; I thought that there was a going away party for me on the other side of the room. Instead, he handed me a pair of Frankenstein shoes to wear home. They were ugly and

I didn't want to wear them. The doctor told me that they would be the only shoes I would be able to wear that would cut down on the pain. The tighter I wore them the better my feet would feel as I walked, not to mention that I couldn't get my feet into my regular shoes.

The cab pulled up to my mother's apartment and all of my friends were standing outside waiting for me to get out. After about 10 minutes I figured out how to get out without putting so much weight on my feet. I tried to act like all was well, but on the inside I wanted everyone to disappear so that I could inch my way to my mom's apartment building without making a spectacle of myself. I really didn't look at anybody, I just made it in the best way I could. I could hear my mother telling my sisters and brothers not to say anything about my shoes because I was just a little sensitive about them at that time.

After a few days, my mother arranged for my sister Crystal and my friend Barbara to get me out of the house and take me for a walk. Maybe the fresh air would do me some good she said. They took me for a few walks but I was moving so slow that they really didn't look like they were enjoying it. So I would just tell them that I was cool and that they didn't have to hang with me.

One of our favorite things to do was go to Maxwell Street—also called "Jew-Town and find bargains with our few dollars. We also liked riding the CTA to get there. It had been about two weeks since I had been home and I was moving a little better. I really wanted to go to this bargain center with my friends but my mother didn't think it was a good idea. They all promised my mother that they would

Recognize

look after me and make sure that I didn't over-do it. I told my mother that most of the trip would be sitting as it took about 30 minutes on the bus to get there. She finally said yes.

There were several abandoned buildings in our neighborhood where the "flashers" would hang out. A flasher is a perverted man who would wear a long black coat with the bottom part to a pair of pants. He gets his kicks from opening his coat and showing his private parts. He would dance around and taunt the young girls while his penis was exposed. Many times he would hold his private part in his hand and swing it up and down and all around and then disappear back into the building.

We got off the bus at Madison and Halsted, and as we walked across the alley the first thing we saw was a flasher. He was standing in the alley and said, "Hey girls." We all knew what he was just by the way he was dressed. They all took off running and left me behind. I had never seen a flasher that close up. He opened his coat and he was naked as a jaybird. I was yelling and screaming "Help, come get me, helllllllp, come get me!" I tried to run, but my feet wouldn't let me. My sister Crystal stopped, looked back at me and was brave enough to come back and help me get away. Then Barbara came. I was small enough where they picked me up by putting their hands under my armpits and took off running with me while my feet were slightly off the ground.

After we were far away from the flasher, we all just looked at each other and laughed. For the next few days they teased me by marking me saying, "Help me, help me, I can't run." I told them that I didn't say, "Help me, help me, I can't run." I said, "Come get me". Either way as I look back, I have to admit, it was funny. We never did tell my mother because we didn't think that she would have found any of it humorous. The more I view the past, the more I realize how valuable it was to have a mother. She showed her love toward me the best she knew how.

I ended up switching schools for my sophomore year. I became captain of pom-pom squad at the new school and helped get our school to the city championship. I met the captain of my old school in the locker room and told her that they could go home because we were going to take the 1st place trophy. We did.

This white wall experience made me recognize that I was borderline illiterate, which is a form of darkness, and that many others in my community were living in darkness as well. I also recognized that girls operated in more jealousy and envy than boys; which I believe is a strategy of Satan to weaken us. We all know that there is strength in numbers. No matter what team we are on in terms of sports, we are all on God's team. We all need to recognize that together we stand and divided we fall.

Recognize

A PRAYER TO COMBAT ILLITERACY AND TO PROMOTE UNITY

Father God please open up my understanding. Touch my mind and allow me to learn how to read, write, and speak the English language. I pray that You would send teachers, monitors, and others who would truly care about my growth, and who would have patience to teach and to educate me. I cancel out illiteracy in my blood line, and in my community, and I call on the spirit of wisdom to over-take me now in the powerful name of Jesus. Lord, I pray that You would unify Your people. Let the strong help the weak and let the weak say that I'm strong. Lord, I bind up the spirit of jealousy and envy right now in Jesus mighty Name, and I loose love, peace, joy, and all the other fruit of the spirit into my territory. In Jesus Name I pray, AMEN!

Meet Homelessness

We had been staying with my grandmother for awhile now. We moved in with her after my mom and dad had their final big fight. My dad had to do some time in the hospital with two stab wounds to the chest.

After about a year, my grandmother moved out, and several months later we moved. We moved to an area where stuff was always going on. Now I was for sure that I wouldn't live to see twenty-five. Either a stray bullet would hit me, I would get beat to death, or some disease would usher me into an early grave. I felt this way because death was always around me. It seemed like an evil force was always within my realm of awareness.

The older I got, the more my mother would despise me. She would always say things like: "You're just like your dad", "You ain't gonna never be sh__, just like your dad." "If you don't get the f__k out of my face, I am going to take you out of this world." I knew that these statements came from the "deep hurt" she felt from her relationship with my father. When she saw me, she saw him.

My worst fear was making my mother mad. The love I knew she had hidden deep down inside was being squashed by so much "rejection" and "unforgiveness." The wiles of Satan made her abort her destiny many years ago. We know that Satan comes to "kill, steal and destroy." I was angry with him because he had targeted my mom and had been successful.

I didn't spend a lot of time at home. I was either at

Recognize

school or at the youth center after school. This would put me in the house around about 9:30 p.m. Since I still had to do my homework, I wouldn't get in the bed until about 11 p.m. I was always very tired.

One of my mother's house rules that each of her girls had was to take a week washing the dishes. When my turn rolled around, I would pay one of my sisters $1 a day to wash dishes for me. They could make $5 for the week if they washed dishes for me the entire week. I didn't have the energy to wash dishes after getting off work and in my heart I felt I shouldn't have had to wash dishes. After all, I reasoned, I didn't really eat anything in the house. My time at the center included many of my meals.

It was my week to do dishes and I told my sister Crystal to do the dishes for me and I would pay her. When I got in from work, I noticed that the dishes were not washed. I woke her up and asked her "Why didn't you do the dishes?" She said, "Shhhh, is mom sleep?" "Yes," I said, "what's up?" "Mom told me that if I wash the dishes for you that she would whip my a--. She said that you think you're too good to wash dishes and that you think you're better than the rest of us. She told me to leave those dishes alone, and that you better wash those dishes or she would kill you." I was in shock! I didn't even eat dinner in that place as I was at school and then at work. Even when food was left on the stove, I didn't want to eat it. We had mice, and I didn't want to take a chance that they had sampled my food first. I should have "recognized" then that she was responding to my pattern of life—not at home like my father, I looked like my father, and sometimes acted like my dad. And, my life was outside of my home most of the time. She wasn't mad at me—she was still mad at my father, I reasoned.

I went ahead and washed the dishes and fell asleep at the kitchen table while trying to read my English assignment. Lucky for me, most of my friends were honor roll students and every book I had to read, they had already read it one or two years prior. I would spend 5 to 10 minutes "picking their brains" for information about each book. In this way, I could pass my oral test at 6th period.

My week of washing dishes rolled around again. I got in the house, looked in the kitchen and saw dishes piled up. I put my school bag down, took off my coat and decided to rest my head before I washed the dishes. I must have been sleep for about three hours. I woke up with a very painful blow to the body. My mother was standing over me with an extension cord. With a look of insanity in her eyes she said, "Get your a-- up and go in there and wash those dishes! You think because you got a little piece of job, you don't have to do sh- - around here, but you are mistaken. You ain't no better than no one else in this house. I don't give a f--k if you never eat a bite in this house, you will have a week of washing the dishes just like everyone else. And, the next time I have to wake you up to wash dishes, you will be sorry, you lazy f--k'n b--ch!"

During this same week, I came in from work and decided to rest my eyes for a few minutes before washing the dishes. Needless to say, I was still sleep when my mother woke up in the middle of the night and she met me with an extension cord blow to the body. I just laid there looking at her. "What are you waiting for, get up!" she yelled.

I didn't want to walk past her with that extension cord in

Recognize

her hand. I was waiting for her to move out of the pathway to the kitchen as she walked back to her bedroom. My sister and brother were trying to comfort me by saying, "Toni, you know how she is. You got to wash the dishes as soon as you come in the house and don't bother lying down. The next time you fall asleep and the dishes are not washed, she may try to kill you."

I called the Magic Man to see what he was up to. He asked about the family, and wanted to know how my mother was doing. I told him about the dishes incident. He told me to just abide by the rules and I would be all right. I really wanted to move in with him but I didn't know how he would take that idea. After all, his girlfriend wasn't liking me too well. She would always tell the Magic Man, "You care about your daughter more than you care about me. You never call me pretty girl, but you call her pretty girl all the time."

I really wanted to live with my dad, because my mother was always "tripping" on me. On the other hand, I didn't want to cramp my father's style.

I made a deal with my sister. I told her that when it was my turn to wash the dishes, all she needed to do was wait until mama went to sleep. Then she could go into the kitchen and wash the dishes for me. My other sister could be on the lookout for when mama was coming. For my other sister's contribution, I would pay her 25 cents. This way, I reasoned, both of my sisters could get paid, the dishes would be washed, I could do my homework, get some rest, and my mother wouldn't have anything to be mad about.

This plan was working for a while until one day I came home and was told how my mother beat the sh-- out of my sister for washing the dishes for me. She told my sister, "If Toni cared anything about you, she wouldn't have had you slaving for her and making you get your a-- kicked!" I felt really sorry for Crystal. She looked like she was in a lot of pain. She had welts everywhere, and it looked like it hurt just to move. I decided to wash my own dishes, even though, (in my sense of justice), I didn't mess any of them up.

The "spirit of anger" is mean and ugly. That is its characteristic. It does not matter who it possesses, it carries out its mission—pain, chaos and anxiety. Its mission is to kill and destroy.

School was school-- classes, pom-pom rehearsals, choir rehearsals, student council meetings and avoiding fights. School was school. Timothy knew I had obligations at school and really needed the job at the center. He wouldn't "trip" when I got there late sometimes. Some days I would get to work in a timely manner, and other times I would be really late. I taught dance to over 80 girls from my neighborhood and girls from a nearby housing complex. Keeping these girls under control was very difficult. I was only 15, and my girls ranged from ages 8 – 13. Many of them were bigger than I was at that time. I put a lot of effort into making them the best in the city. We won several local dance competitions, and they began to take pride in being apart of something nice for a change.

As captain of pom-pom girls in high school, we always were in the running if not on top. My dancing abilities came naturally. Even though I hadn't had any professional dance lessons, I was doing well. All of my dance creations came from the soul. Most of my dances, whether at the center or

Recognize

at school, were created in my head from watching stuff on TV coupled with a lot of street dance moves. Most of my moves were hard, powerful, bold, and energetic. As a dance instructor at the center, I couldn't do my homework there. I had to wait until I got home.

Today was a rough day: Drama at school, teaching the girls about non-violence at the center, and trying to keep up with all of my assignments. Now, to top things off, another week of dishes. It started to feel like my turn was coming around every other week even though the interval was every four weeks. As I entered our small one bedroom apartment, everyone was already in the bed. One of my sister's got up and said, "Don't forget it's your turn to wash dishes, and mama already warned us that anyone who feels like getting their a-- whipped tonight will wash dishes for Toni."

I didn't want any of my sisters to get in trouble, so I decided not to come up with any other great ideas or a plan that would put my sisters in harm's way. The only plan I had was to rest for a few minutes, get up and do the dishes, do my homework, and go to bed.

The sharp, angry voice of my mother woke me out of my sleep. "B--ch, you think I'm playing with you. I told you the next time you fall asleep without washing those dishes, I would kill you." My mother was standing over me with a butcher knife. Before I could move out of her way, she was coming down toward my neck with the knife.

The commotion awakened the whole house. My brother Michael grabbed her arms and was trying to get the knife out of her hand. My mother was screaming "Let me go, I'm going to kill this b--ch." I was trying to get out of the way.

96

I didn't know what to do. It was now clear that she meant what she said. She wanted to get me bad. I didn't know if I should just run into the kitchen and begin washing the dishes or if I should just run back outside away from death. My sisters and brothers kept telling me to leave. I ran for the door.

I couldn't tell what time of night it was. I didn't know what to do or where to go. It could have been 1:00 o'clock in the morning. I didn't have any money on me to call my dad and I didn't have any place to go. So I walked the streets for a while talking junk with the neighborhood prostitutes until I got tired, and then I sneaked into the hallway of my mother's building and slept there for the night.

When morning came, I knocked on the door as slowly as I could to see if one of my sisters would come to the door. I needed to get my book bag and workout clothes. No one answered. Then, I went outside into the alley near the window where the bedroom was. I picked up a few small rocks and threw them at the window in hopes to get one of my sisters to come to the window. My sister Crystal was always there. I asked her, "Where is mama?" "I think she's still sleep," Crystal said. "Do you think it's safe for me to come back in?" Crystal replied, "I don't think so. Mama said if any of us let you in, she would kill us." "I said, "OK, just hand me my book and gym bag." She disappeared out of the window. I was hoping that she wouldn't get busted.

My bags came flying down without any warning. I didn't get a chance to say thank you. She had disappeared that quickly. I went to school as if it was another day. As I walked to work, I was wondering where I would sleep tonight. Times

Recognize

were just flying by, and it got later and later. Timothy told me to go home, that he would finish up and lock up. I went into the gym room instead of going outside. I thought staying inside the center would be better than sleeping outside.

I heard him leaving as he turned out the lights. The center wasn't the same in the middle of the night. It was spooky. I even saw some rats running around. I didn't know the center had rats. I was locked inside the youth center. I didn't know if I was going to make it through the night. I was hungry, scared, nervous, and wishing I was at home in bed. I sat up all night keeping my eyes on the activities of the rats in the center. I was determined not to go to sleep.

I finally succumbed to sleep. Suddenly I felt something on my leg! I woke up screaming as I thought that a big fat rat was trying to climb up my leg! Instead it was Timothy. It was daylight and time for the center to open. "What are you doing here?" he asked. "I didn't have any place to go," I said, "so I thought it would be a good idea to stay here." "It's not safe for you to stay in the center at night like this. Go to school, and we'll talk about this later on this evening." One of the daytime directors told Timothy that I was in the gym room sleep and that he needed to come see about me.

I got to school early enough to have breakfast. I went through my day as normal. When I got to the center, Timothy wanted to see me in his office. He wanted to know what was going on with me. He inquired whether I could stay with a relative or something. After I told Timothy what happened with the dishes and the knife scene, he told me he would handle everything. He told me to go to the gym room and start my dance class with the girls. Timothy told me he had a talk with my mother, but had no luck in dealing with her. He wouldn't tell me what happened. He just said, he knew a girl who came there to play ball who had her own apartment. Maybe, he thought, I could stay with her for awhile.

Because our household lacked salvation, the hedge of protection that should have been there for both me and my mother, had been broken. There were all kinds of spirits operating in my household. My mother was so disappointed with the likes of my father, that bitterness and anger had an easy entrance to her soul. Satan is so crafty that he took this scenario to try to prescribe me an early death. For some reason Satan didn't want me around. I guess because he knew that one day I would be used by God to tear down his kingdom. The spirit of anger that was operating in my mother was designed to destroy the both of us. Although I didn't know how to war against the devil, God sent His angels to care for me until I was spiritually mature enough to fight back.

Recognize

A PRAYER OF PROTECTION
FOR THE HOMELESS

Father God everyone isn't homeless by choice; please protect every homeless child, teen, and innocent person who has found themselves out on the street with no place to turn. Protect their going and their coming. Provide a way out of no way. Cover them with Your blood and keep them from all hurt, harm, and danger. In Jesus Name I pray, AMEN.

Meet Gail

"Toni meet Gail. Gail meet Toni," Timothy said. "Gail, Toni needs a place to stay and I know you have your own place. She's a nice girl and she works here all year round. Do you have enough space for her?" "Sure, I have a three-bedroom apartment. My dad gave it to me when I turned 16," she informed us. "Wow! You have your own three-bedroom apartment? How much do you pay for rent?" I asked. "I don't pay anything. My dad and mom own the building, and it's paid for." "Whaaaat??!! Y'all must be rich!" "I wouldn't say all that," Gail said.

"What's up with your folks?" Gail asked. "Well, my mother is under a little stress. She is trying to raise seven kids on public aid, and my dad left us and is now living with his girl friend. I'm looking for a place to stay because it's not enough room at my mom's place." (I didn't want to tell her that I'd been kicked out after my mother tried to kill me. That just didn't sound right.)

"Well, I'm going to the gym to play ball, what time do you get off work?" Gail asked. "I get off at 9 p.m." "Cool," Gail continued, "I'll stop back up here and get you. My man is going to pick me up, and you can ride with us. "Cool." I said.

Gail was two years older than I was. She was 18, and I was 16. She had 15 brothers and sisters, and she was the youngest of them all. She called her mother and father by their first names-Eugene and Ruby. Gail was very carefree, and was always happy. She also had a lot of friends. She didn't get high, but loved to go out partying. Even though she was at the age to go to college, she felt like she didn't have to.

Recognize

She had everything she wanted and didn't want to waste her time and/or money going to college.

I was sitting in Timothy's office when Gail came to get me. "You ready?" she asked. Yes! I couldn't wait to get to her place and take a shower, and rest my head in a bed for a change. "Meet me downstairs" she said. When I got downstairs, she was in a car with two boys: One in the front with her and one sitting in the back. "Toni, this is my man Dallas, and this is his friend Tyrell." "Why are you standing there looking crazy, get in." Gail said. As I opened the door to get into the car, I was thinking that the car looked like it needed to be in the junk yard, and that I didn't want to be bothered with some boy at this time of night. I was tired, hungry, and needed to get my homework done.

"Damn, you fine!" Tyrell said. "Thank you." "Gail said you were cute. Do you have a boyfriend?" "No I don't!" "What type of sh-- are you into?" "I'm not into no type of sh--." I said it with a slight attitude. "Okay, Okay, I'll quit cursing," Tyrell said. "Let's start over. What type of things do you like to do?" "I don't like to do nothing." "Damn Gail, your girl ain't nothing like you. She's like a cold a-- popsicle." "Tyrell, just chill!" Gail said. "She just needs to warm up to you that's all." I just sat there in the car hoping that Tyrell's arm or leg wouldn't touch me.

As we approached Gail's place, I saw two stray dogs. One was brownish red with a little blonde on the legs, and the other was black and white. I couldn't tell what type of dogs they were because they were mutts. But, they were both pretty large. Both dogs had hair missing in spots as if they had a disease, and they were walking up on everyone that walked by to sniff them.

The building was big. It was a three flat, six unit brick building with lots of kids outside. I thought that it was strange to have so many kids outside this time of night. It was 10 p.m. The building was dark. It was a dirty brown brick building that hadn't been tuck-pointed in years. Many of the windows were boarded up, and the others had bed sheets for curtains.

Before I got out of the car I asked Gail if those were her dogs. She said, "No, they are my sister's dogs, but they won't bite." When we got out of the car, both dogs came running over to us. I almost climbed on Gail's back. "Damn girl, I told you that the dogs are not going to bite you! With the way you're acting, I might bite your a-- my damn self." Everyone within hearing distance started laughing, Dallas, Tyrell, and all the kids. I told Gail that I didn't like dogs. When I was about 12 years old I got bit by my neighbor's German Shepherd. I can remember that dog trying to take my leg off. I still have the scars to prove it.

Gail said, "As long as you don't f--k with these dogs they won't f--k with you. So, just walk natural because they can sense fear. And with your scary a-- they probably are looking at you like you are their lunch." "I'm not scary," I murmured, "I just don't like dogs."

As we got closer to the building, I could smell something. It smelled like doo-doo. "What's that smell?" I asked. "Just watch your step. Sometimes the dogs sh-- in the hallway and my sister and her old man take forever cleaning it up. My dad keeps saying he's going to put my sisters out, but he's too sickly to fool with my sisters and their drug addict boyfriends.

Recognize

Gail lived on the first floor across from her mom and dad. The other four units, two on each floor, were occupied by four of her sisters and their boyfriends and kids. None of the sisters were married to their live-in-boyfriends.

The hallway was very dark. As I tried to feel my way up the stairs to her apartment, I stepped on something. The object began to move. It was another dog! Gail told me that Ben (the dog) likes to sleep on the third step from the top. She told me to be sure to skip that step when coming in and out. I was holding on to Tyrell's arm so tight, I know he wasn't able to feel any blood in his hand. He didn't seem to mind. I think he was getting a kick out of the fact that I went from a "cold a-- popscicle" to a needy damsel in distress.

As she opened her front door, I could see that her apartment was pretty nice. She had ok carpet, a nice couch and a 19" color TV. Her bedroom was also nice, but the other two bedrooms were empty. Her kitchen was very nasty, and her back door did not look safe. It looked like someone had kicked it in. The glass was missing and it was replaced with plastic and masking tape. The door had three pieces of wood nailed across it to keep it shut. In case of an emergency, you would have been out of luck trying to get out of the back door.

"Where's the bathroom?" I asked. She pointed to a door that said "KEEP OUT!" "Why does it say keep out?" I innocently inquired. "Because that's what you need to do," she answered in a tone I had not heard from her. All of a sudden, a black cat walked by me. "I thought you said that you didn't have any pets?" I said. "I told you that I didn't have any dogs," Gail replied. "This is Black Night. Say hi to Toni," Gail said to the cat.

Dallas was calling Gail from the bedroom. She told him she would be right back. She ran out the house and was gone for about 20 minutes and went straight into the bedroom with Dallas when she returned. In the meantime, I wanted to go into the bathroom but it said KEEP OUT! So, I went into the living room, sat on the couch next to Tyrell and told him that I needed to do my homework. He said that he thought we were going to get to know each other a little better. I told him maybe some other time, but in my mind I was thinking "I know he don't think I'm going to give up the pooh-nan-naay!"

As I sat there and did my homework, Black Night walked into the living room, stood by the front door and just screamed. It wasn't a meow, it was an ungodly scream. That cat looked over at us with his back arched, with his sharp teeth showing, and just looked like he was possessed. Tyrell looked at me and said, "Damn girl, what's up with you? I have never seen that cat do that before." "What makes you think he's doing that to me. He may just want to go outside." "Hell naw!" Tyrell said with confidence. "That cat got nothing but hate for you. I'm out of here." Tyrell left.

Gail was in her bedroom with her man. I was in the living room. Once I was done with my homework, I laid on the couch, and went to sleep with the TV on. I tried really hard to stay up because I didn't trust that black cat.

The next morning Dallas went home and Gail ran upstairs. I waited until I got to school to brush my teeth. After school, I went to the center. Timothy wanted to know how were things over at Gail's house. I told him, "It beats sleeping outside." But I really wasn't telling the entire truth.

Recognize

It was about the same as sleeping outside.

Another night and another evening at Gail's place. I really needed to use the bathroom and Gail had gone out with one of her men to get something to eat. I never moved off the couch in Gail's living room because it appeared to be the safest place in the entire building. I couldn't hold my bladder any longer so something had to be done. As I got up off the couch, I noticed that the only light on in the house was the light from the TV, everything else was dark and scary. I went over to the door that said KEEP OUT, (the taped up bathroom). I then put my ear up to the door to see if I could hear anything, then I removed the tape, and took one step into the room. I almost lost my balance, but I took hold of the doorknob. Thank God I did, because there was no floor in the bathroom. No nothing! The room was completely empty and the floor was gone. If I had let go of the doorknob I would have ended up in the basement of the building.

As the doorknob broke my fall, I could hear something moving around in the basement. My imagination kicked in. Had I awakened some big monster that was going to come up from the basement? Would it kill me, and no one would know where to find my body? I quickly closed the door and taped it back up.

There was a knock at the front door. Who is it? I thought—another strange happening in the Twilight Zone? It was Tyrell. Oh, back to reality. Perhaps Tyrell at the door was worse than a monster. I really didn't like Tyrell, but I was so glad to see him. He was looking for Dallas, but he wasn't there. I told Tyrell to come in, and told him about my experience with the bathroom door. He wanted to show his bravery so he walked to the back to Gail's kitchen, got a flashlight and proceeded to the bathroom door. What are you doing?" I asked. He said that he wanted to see what was down in the basement. He removed the tape, opened the door, and pointed the flashlight toward the basement. We saw stuff moving around. There were rats! Rats everywhere. It was like a big fat rat factory. It was the most gross thing I had ever seen.

Tyrell was taken by surprise as much as I was. So much so that he accidentally dropped the flashlight into the pool of rats, and the rats began to scatter. Tyrell said, "I'm out of here." I told him not to leave me, but he did. About 10 minutes later Gail and Dallas returned. I didn't mention anything about what had happened. I just wanted to find a way to tell Gail I was leaving, but I first needed to figure out where I would go next.

I still had to empty my bladder, and the pain in my bladder was getting worse. "Gail, Gail," I yelled as I knocked on her bedroom door. "What?!" she responded impatiently. "I need to use it," I said, "where should I go?" She yelled back, "Go up to one of my sister's apartments, and ask them if you can use their bathroom." I really didn't want to go into the hall. It was dark, and I couldn't see which steps the dogs were on, and I didn't like them walking up on me. As I built up my courage and as the pain grew worse and worse in my bladder, I went into the hallway. I finally made it to the second floor. I knocked on the first door I could get to. A voice yelled from the inside, "WHO IS IT?!!" "It's me, Toni, I need to use the bathroom."

"One of you little mother F------s let that girl in." About 10 kids came to the door. They were all dirty and patting my

Recognize

pockets for money. I really wanted to knock them down, but instead, I said "No, no, don't do that!" I walked to the bathroom as it was in the same spot as in Gail's place. I opened the door, and rubbed the wall for a light switch, but instead I got a hand full of sticky stuff. Oddly enough, I didn't feel a light switch. So I decided to just walk over to the toilet and just stand over it and pee. I didn't want to take a chance of touching something I would regret down the road.

As I reached for the dark covered toilet seat, it began to get lighter. I couldn't tell what was going on. I became more determined to find a light switch. As I walked to the middle of the bathroom, I could feel a string hanging from the ceiling. I pulled on it and the light came on. I looked at the toilet seat and there were so many roaches on the seat that it looked like a seat cover made out of live roaches. I became sick to my stomach. I took a dirty towel and waved the roaches away. I stood over the toilet and emptied my bladder. I ran out of that apartment and knew right at that moment that I really needed to find another place to stay.

There was an odd spirit in that entire building. I think it was the spirit of poverty. I sensed many other spirits there, but the dominant one was the spirit of poverty. The dogs, the feces, the roaches and the rats were all manifestations of those runaway spirits which had overtaken that building. My challenge in later life was if this spirit, which prevailed in many of the communities of my youth, could be recognized and then uprooted. Could civil rights and other social and black movement issues of the time really be "spiritual?"

I called Steve. He worked at the youth center with me, and always had a listening ear. Steve really wanted to help me, but really couldn't do much. He lived with his sanctified mother and seven brothers. His father was dead, he had killed himself two years prior to my meeting Steve. Steve was always listening to my horror stories and wishing he could help. He was able to pick me up from Gail's house and drop me off in front of my mother's building. I felt safer sleeping in my mother's hallway instead of in a roach infested, rat infested, cat and dog infested dark, haunted, kid infested building. I did finally stay a few nights with Steve—the details of which must come at a later time.

Cleanliness is next to godliness. A building filled with rats, mice, and roaches are a sign of unclean spirits living with you or in your territory. You can be poor but yet clean, or clean and yet have ungodly creatures residing with you. Recognize what's going on around you and your territory, and seek deliverance. I've noticed that many unsaved people are more prone to rodents. In Gail's situation, she and her sisters were living out a generational curse. All of her sisters had five or more kids by different men, and all of them were on some type of public assistance. It appeared that they were all sentenced to live a life that was beneath and not above. Even in my homelessness, I could recognize the curses, the demons, and the unclean spirits, that were operating around me.

Recognize

A PRAYER OF DELIVERANCE
FOR THE UNSAVED

Father God in the Name of Jesus, I confess with my mouth and I believe in my heart that Jesus is Lord and ruler over my life. I denounce every curse that is assigned to my life and I choose You Lord on this day. I pray that You clean out my heart, my life, and my household, and fill every area of my life with Your Holy Spirit. Teach me Lord how to walk in Your ways and how to live a life of Holiness. Lead and guide me to a church that will help me grow, and bring me closer to You. I want to be more like You in all my ways. Thank You Lord for saving me, in Jesus Name I pray. AMEN!

Meet my Dad's place

I was at a nearby pay phone near my mother's house. I needed to call my dad to see if I could kick it with him for a little while. "Where are you?" he asked. "I'm at a pay phone by the expressway. Can you come get me?" "Why don't I just call your mother and ask her to let you come home?" "You can, but I don't think you can talk her into anything. You're not one of her favorite people." "You got a point," he said, "I'll be out to get you in a few hours. Be in front of the building. I just have to work a few things out and I'll come get you." I think it took him about three hours to get me. I was sleep on the ground when he pulled up. He blew his horn. I got up and got into his car. "What's up halfpint?" "Nothing, I'm just tired and ready to go to bed," I said. "I almost didn't recognize you, you looked like a little rag doll laying on the ground." "Well, I feel like a rag doll." "Well, I can't help the way your mother treats you. You just need to stay out of trouble and out of her way, and things would work out for you."

I was too tired for rebuttal, but I wanted to say that if you hadn't left her/us, she wouldn't be bitter and taking her frustration out on me. I stopped talking hoping he would just let us ride in silence. After about 30 minutes, he said, "We're here." He lived in a three flat building that looked like no one paid the light bill. We had to walk half-way around the building to get in. After getting in, I just flopped down on the couch and fell asleep. About 4 o'clock in the morning, I could hear his girlfriend asking why does your daughter need to be here. And, she added, if I was going to be there for any length of time, I would have to pay my way by washing dishes,

Recognize

or cleaning up or doing something to help out. Three hours later, I got up to get ready for school and my dad asked me if I could wash the dishes before I left for school. Oh, not dishes again!

I looked around his small kitchen and there was old Chinese food out, old pizza boxes, dishes in the sink up to the ceiling and for the most part it looked like they hadn't washed dishes since the day they moved in. Dead roaches were floating in the old dish water and the smell of spoiled stuff covered the entire kitchen. I felt like an evil stepmother was trying to make me her slave girl. I told my dad that if I had to wash all those dishes it would make me late for school. "OK fine, let's go so I can get you to school in time." As I got out of the car, my dad yelled, "What time do I need to pick you up from work?" "9:00," I shouted as I ran into the school, giving myself a half hour of cush time as my dad was always running late.

My dad picked me up from work and took me back to his apartment. I was hoping that his unemployed girlfriend had taken a few hours out of her "business" schedule to clean that kitchen, but as my luck would have it, the kitchen was still nasty. When I got in, I made myself comfortable on the couch, did my homework, and was trying to get ready for bed. It was about 10:30 p.m. and I needed to take a bath and go to sleep. Now enters the wicked witch of the west. "Can you wash those dishes before you go to bed?" "Why should I wash the dishes if I didn't mess them up? (That argument was familiar to me). I don't even eat here, plus there are way too many dishes in that sink for me to wash by myself. What I can do is help you wash the dishes, or maybe even teach you how to keep the kitchen clean."

Now I knew that statement would launch the war. "I know you are not trying to get smart with me?" she said with the most indignant tone she could muster. She stormed out the front room and started to make life miserable for my dad. My dad came in the front and asked me to try to get along with his woman. He told me that he would pay me if I would wash the dishes. (Now this way of getting the dishes washed sounded strangely familiar.) I told him if he could find me some safety gloves I would wash the dishes.

Now there was a colony of roaches in the sink—as many roaches as there were dishes. After he found me a pair of gloves, I washed the dishes just to keep the peace, and then I went to bed. My dad and his woman would argue every night. He had changed women but not the "at home" conversations. I didn't know if it was because of me, or part of his script in life, but to keep peace from my end of it and to give my dad his life back, I told him that he didn't have to pick me up anymore. Somehow, I would make it. Homeless, shameless and somewhat blameless—I lived in the streets.

Satan was trying to destroy me with the spirit of rejection which is attached to other spirits like loneliness, anger, and low self-esteem. I loved my mom, but I knew that she needed her space, so I wasn't trying to step to her. I loved my dad, but he didn't know how to be a dad, so he was trying to be a friend on some level. When I was down in my spirit I would just say to myself "that there is someone on this planet that is worse off than me." The spirit of rejection can cause you to run to people you don't need to be around, and put you into situations that you don't need to be in, so beware of the spirit of rejection and protect your heart from all hurtful and harmful situations.

Recognize

A PRAYER FOR THE REJECTED

Father God I know it's better to have You with me, even if the whole world is against me. Lord, keep me in Your perfect peace as my mind is stayed on You. Lord I know that You don't make mistakes. I stand on Your Word in Psalm 139:14 that says I am fearfully and wonderfully made. Lord as I walk through the valley of the shadow of death, I will fear no evil, for You are with me. Lord I see Your footprints in the sand, and I thank You for carrying me, when I couldn't walk on my own. Fill me with Your Holy Ghost Power so that I will be able to withstand the fiery darts of the evil one. Help me to love those who use me and spitefully abuse me. Bless my friends, family, and enemies. I submit all of my problems, my hurts, and disappointments to You Lord, and I will not let the evil one in. Please send Your warrior angel Michael to see after me, and protect me from the evil one in Your Son Jesus' name I pray, AMEN!

Meet Joann and Shug

Joann and Shug lived on my block in the same court way building as my mother. Joann was about 24 and Shug was about 21. These sisters were hookers. I was about sixteen when I was out in the street and when I needed to take a quick nap Joann and Shug would watch over me.

Joann and Shug were both really dark skinned. Joann was prettier than Shug in my opinion. She was tall, I would say about five feet seven inches, but her hooker boots would make her look taller. She had even, smooth skin and pretty white teeth. She always wore a lot of makeup, which took away from her beauty. She had very long legs and always had on a skirt that showed part of her booty. She wore a wig that was long black and shiny. Sometimes her wig looked like it needed to be combed and washed out. She always looked like she had an attitude and always carried a knife in her boot. Every jacket she wore had fake fur around the collar and it would always look dirty and nappy.

In the summer, they both wore halter tops and daisy dukes (very short shorts). Joann would walk with long strides and always had a Virginia Slim cigarette in her mouth. I had never seen her smile. She always wore a straight serious look on her face. Any time you would see Joann, she was looking up and down the street as if she was waiting for a cab and had to get somewhere in a hurry. She always had cars picking her up. She wasn't out on the street as much as Shug. I guess her skills were keeping her quite busy.

Shug, on the other hand, was much smaller than Joann. She was about five feet four inches, and was always fighting

Recognize

with someone. She dated a drug dealer, and she always looked like she was high. Her skin was black and ashy. She had a few missing teeth and the ones that she did have were beige. She wore boots also with a short black leather skirt with a matching leather jacket. She wore a wig that was short and slightly curly, and big hoop earrings. Shug was always running from the police or one of her 'tricks.'

Men would come around looking for Shug wanting to know what apartment she lived in. I would always say, "I didn't know." I didn't want to be in the middle of Shug's drama. Shug would come out late at night and ask me if anyone was looking for her. I would tell her who and when, and she would look very nervous and uneasy after talking to me. I never knew why Shug was always in trouble and always on the run.

Shug and her boyfriend were always fighting. He would call her all kinds of terrible names and she would throw a broken glass bottle at him, or whatever she could get her hands on and take off running. One quiet summer evening, I was sitting in the doorway of the building in my normal sleeping quarters (I wasn't allowed in the house). I happened to notice someone standing over me. It was Joann. She was just standing there looking down at me, not saying a word. She slowly took out a cigarette, lit it, and took a puff. All while this is going on, I wondered, what is her problem? She finally asked me, "Do you know how to braid hair?" I said, "Yes," she bargained, "I will pay you to braid my hair, so when I return, be ready!" Her words were always firm and straight to the point. She looked me over one last time, took another puff off of her cigarette, looked both ways down the street, and took off in those long strides in a very fast pace. She was always walking like she was late for some very important meeting.

Joann returned later in the evening and took her boot and shook me as I slept outside. "Are you ready?" she asked. I almost forgot what she was talking about. "Yes, yes, yes, I'm ready," I said after I was fully awake. "Where should we go?" "Come with me," she said. She took me to her apartment. She lived with Shug and her mother who was very sickly. Joann put the key in the door, and I heard a small feeble voice ask, "Joann is that you?" Joann answered back and said, "Yes, Madear. Joann told me to take a seat and wait in the living room for her."

The place was nasty. Clothes were piled up in every corner. The carpet was worn, dirty, and smelled like old smoke. Everything in the house was old, and the lights were so very dim. The atmosphere was almost that of a haunted house. They had several wig heads sitting around with different styled wigs hanging on them. The couch I was sitting on looked like it was a flower print, but it was so dirty, I couldn't make out what it was. Sitting on the mantle were family pictures and pictures of Joann and Shug in there graduation caps and gowns. They both looked so pretty and happy. I started wondering what my graduation day would be like. How would I end up? Like Joann and Shug? I imagine that no one is thinking, that after I graduate, that I would want to be a hooker. I wanted to know how did this happen to Joann and Shug. I knew that someday I would find out.

Joann asked me if I wanted anything to drink. I couldn't imagine the house having any clean glasses. All I could think about was swallowing a roach, or even worse, swallowing some

Recognize

roach eggs that would live in my stomach until hatching and one day they would all come running out of my ears and nose. I politely said, "No thank you." She proceeded to pull off her wig. She looked so extremely different with her wig off. Her hair was middle length, very nappy, and bald around the edges. She told me if I did a good job, she would let me braid her hair on a regular basis. I started taking the braids down that she already had in her head. Her hair smelled horrible. It was a mixture of smoke and old sweat from wearing the wigs all the time. I was guessing too, perhaps the smell of bad sex.

I asked her if she wanted me to wash her hair first, and she said that she didn't have time for all of that. "If I wanted my hair washed, I would have asked you to wash it, just do what I asked you to do," she said. "Okay fine. Don't bite my head off!" She turned around and looked at me for a long time as if to say, you better watch your mouth, but instead, she didn't say a word. Then, I broke the silence, "I need you to turn around, so I can get done with your hair."

As I combed her hair, the teeth from the comb began to fly across the room. "Damn girl watch it! You're about to pull all of my hair out of my f--k'n head." "Sorry." I didn't want to make her mad, so I took my time untangling her hair as to not break anymore of the teeth in her comb. I then oiled her scalp and neatly braided her hair. All while I braided her hair, she lit cigarette after cigarette. I asked her if she could wait until I was done to smoke because I couldn't take the smell of that smoke going directly from her cigarette right into my nose. She asked me why should she put her cigarette out. I told her because I felt like I was about to die from smoke inhalation. "Well B-----, we all have to go somehow!" She continued to smoke. An hour later, I was done.

Joann walked over to the drawer, and moved the stockings that were hanging over the mirror to examine my work. She finally said, "Not bad." She handed me $20 and told me she would let me know when she needed it redone. Both Joann and Shug became regular customers. While braiding their hair, I would hear about all of their "tricks." I finally found out why Shug was always on the run. The police were looking for her all the time because she would do drug drops for her man. Joann would always cuss her out and tell her she was a stupid black B-----. She would tell Shug to let him do his own drug drops

Shug was also a thief. She would always try to rob her customers while they were asleep. She was very successful on many occasions, but when she got caught, she would get a royal beating. She had many nicks and cuts in her face. "Part of the job," she said with an attitude. I really didn't like braiding Shug's hair. It was more nappy than Joann's. Both heads, however, were equally smelly. She had a little gray hair and it was very fragile. Her hair was past dirty. It was filthy! When I combed it, dust would fly in my face. And to make matters worse, after I was done braiding her hair, she would sometimes say, "I will pay you later."

I never had the heart to ask them why they had become hookers. I could tell from being around them that they felt like it was quick fast money and it paid the bills. I really felt sorry for Joann and Shug. They were working the streets to pay rent, and to take care of their sick mother. What legitimate jobs were available on the Westside which could accomplish that?

Recognize

I wondered if their mother knew where they were getting all of that cash from. They both spoke very sweetly around their mother, and were like little angels. But, when they were out of her hearing range, they were like little demons. I said to myself, 'she must be an awesome woman to have her daughters under that kind of control' (under control as far as she knew.)

Joann was coming out of her mother's bedroom as I was coming into the apartment. I could hear her saying, "Yes Madear, I will see if Toni could do something with your hair." She was using her angel voice. Joann walked into the kitchen to empty a tray that her mother had earlier. Then she walked into the living room where I was standing, and in her demon voice said, "After you do my hair, I want you to braid my mother's hair and I"ll pay you." I said, "Cool."

Finally Joann asked me to wash her hair. As I had her "under the sink," I asked her what made her pick her line of work. She told me none of my f—k'n business. I decided not to bring it up again. I would ask Shug. She seemed to like telling me, teaching me and giving vivid details. We walked into Joann's bedroom. She got a chair and put it in front of the mirror so she could watch me do her hair. At one point we were both looking in the mirror at each other. "What the F--- you looking at?" Joann asked. "I'm looking at you." Joann had a bad attitude, and I wasn't in the mood for her today, so I didn't back down. She said, "I know you're looking at me because you think I'm a ho! But one day you'll be selling your pussy for money too." I said, "That's a lie!" "That's what you say now, but when you get hungry and tired of sleeping in the streets, you will let some man suck your breast, look at your body, and get some of that cat for some cash."

I looked at her through the mirror with eyes of hate. I hated her for saying that. I told her that I would never sell my body for money. She said "Never say never." She pinched my nipple and walked away. Shug walked in on the middle of our conversation as Joann was on her way out. Shug said, "Toni don't listen to that bitter B-----. She is always talking like she is some queen bee. Now I must say, God didn't give you those big breasts for nothing, but you don't have to be a ho. Go to college and make something of yourself. Hell, somebody in this neighborhood need to." Just because Joann and I f--ked up, don't mean you need to. Maybe if you get a big job working for a big company and you become the big boss, I can come work for you. I'm tired of this street bull sh--! Joann is too. She is just trying to pretend that she is all that."

Joann was on her way out the door. She stopped in front of me and said, "You can put your dancing skills with your big breasts and make big money shaking for the men." As she tried to reach for my left breast to pinch it again, I blocked her just in time and she felt the knife I had tucked in my jeans as her arm fell down to my side. "What's this?" she asked. "My knife. I keep it on me at all times. You never know when you have to use it." "Do you know how to use it?" she asked. "Yes, I know how to use it." She whipped out her knife from her boot and said, "Show me." I whipped mine out of my pants and held it in front of me. She said, "Not bad, a little slow, but not bad. I have one tip for you baby girl, never, ever pull out your knife or any other weapon unless you plan on using it. I don't care how bad you are getting your a-- kicked, only pull out your knife if you really have to, and plan on using it. People don't take you serious if you pull out a knife and not use it, so if you are going to

Recognize

carry a knife you have to know the rules. I'm out of here. Don't forget to do my mother's hair. Bye you hoes!" She had now included me as an honorary member of the infamous sorority as she walked out the door.

I walked into her mother's room. It was dark, and it felt like the death angel had taken up residency. She was short, skinny, and old looking. I really couldn't guess her age, because of her sickness. She said, "Come on in baby," She didn't have any tubes or IVs or anything that would give me an indication of her illness. All she had was a drug store full of medicine on her dusty night stand. "Do you need me to help you sit up?" I asked. She said, "No, just give me a minute." "Do you like it this dark in here?" I asked. She said, "Well, I don't know." Her voice was so sad. So I went ahead and opened up the curtain in her room. I even threw out some of the trash that was building up in every corner. As I combed her hair, I couldn't find anything to talk to her about. She was quiet and so was I.

"Do you work with my girls?" she asked. "No, Mam," I said. I wondered if she knew where her daughters worked. What did they tell her? What was I to do or say? She said, "Good! You look like a good girl, you'll have many options in life." At this point, I knew that she knew. I didn't know what to say. I knew in my heart she was sad about her situation, and about having two daughters as hookers. She started to hum a church hymn- Amazing Grace.

Toward the middle of the song I started humming with her. She put her hand on my hand as we hummed together. I could feel her pain, and I think she could feel mine. At that moment, she needed me as a daughter, and I needed her as a mother. That song brought a certain level of healing to both of us. She was surprised that I knew the lyrics to the song, but my grandmother used to sing hymns all the time. She, after all, was a soprano in the Senior Choir. It seems that a lot of the things that my grandmother had taught me earlier in life have come back to my memory—as if God Himself had an interest in my well-being and has expressed it in the recollections of a blessed childhood or Sunday school and choirs and "playing church." Church, and the need for it, was now somehow real—and urgent!

Was there another spirit at work here? Had the Spirit seen the hurt of a mother recognizing the demons, but having no knowledge as to how to battle them? Would I ever be in a position to war against these destroyers of hope, these robbers of joy? Would God allow me such an opportunity?

After a few minutes of silence, the old lady said, "One day God is going to answer my prayers and get my daughters off the streets. You don't have to tell me, I know where quick fast money comes from. If I would have just gone ahead and died, my girls wouldn't have to live like this. I know things have got to be better on the other side." All of a sudden, I could feel her deep pain. I knew that she knew. I knew she was not only sick but also unhappy. I knew she wasn't enjoying life anymore. I knew she wanted her daughters to give up the street life. However, there was nothing she could do about it. I wanted to pray, but I didn't know how. I wanted to hug her, but I didn't know how. I wanted to encourage her, but I didn't know how. So, I just remained silent.

I continued to comb her hair softly, oiled it, braided it and handed her a mirror. She stared at that mirror as if it

Recognize

was the first time she had ever seen her own image. She smiled and said, "Thank you." She was so defeated in her situation that she had given up on her own life and on the life of her daughters. Satan was on his job—he was killing, stealing and destroying. It felt like the devil was winning all the battles.

But she had been seeing through a "darkened glass." Could it be that God would send me to replace that medicine on her night stand with the hope of Jesus? Would God give me the tools to straighten not only hair—but heads? I prayed that I might be His messenger. Joann had already paid me for doing her mother's hair before she went to work. Her mother, however, insisted on paying me. She said, "Baby, look in my top drawer over there and bring me that old hat box." She opened the hatbox and handed me about six pieces of peppermint candy. I didn't know if she was trying to tell me my breath was "kicking," or this was all she had to pay me. I told her that Joann had taken care of her bill. She said that she didn't want Joann or Shug's money. Their money was from the devil. She wanted to pay for her own hair and all she had was a bag of peppermint candy. I took the candy as she wished, but I also kept the $20. That $20 was much needed. I would learn later that "the wealth of the wicked is reserved for the righteous."

Shug was very playful when she was high. She would always pull on my breasts and say, "I need these big breasts then I could up my price." I asked Shug what made her turn to the street. All she could say was, "Sh—happens." I was still mad from what Joann said to me earlier about one day I would be selling my body. I made up in my mind that day that no matter what, I would never sell my body for money. I sometimes think of Joann and wonder why she was so introspective. Why was she always staring into space? What had a hold of her? Why was she so sad and distant? I saw her looking in the mirror one day at herself and she was wiping away her tears. She was sad and caught up in her situation. Shug was too high to realize she was caught up. She had escaped, like many, into the demon of addiction.

I remember from reading my Bible that Jesus would forgive anyone who confessed their sins. He would say, "Your sins are forgiven, go and sin no more". Joann or Shug never talked about Jesus, and I didn't know how to witness. I was just hoping that God had something else in store for me. I also prayed that Joann and Shug would remain safe.

I didn't want to be like Joann or Shug, so I started adding to my nightly prayer, "Lord, please, whatever you do, please, please don't let me be a hooker." When I think of Joann and Shug, I remember their graduation picture there hanging on their mantle. I know that they didn't plan to work the streets either, and live such a hard life. During the 70s when people didn't have an explanation for things happening they would just say, "S--- HAPPENS!" I wanted to know how?

Many times cars would pull up thinking I worked with Joann and Shug and wanted to offer me money. Joann would just pull out her blade not saying a word and give them the look of death. The driver would read her non-verbal language and just drive off. Anytime Shug was around and I got propositioned, she would first joke around and ask me if I wanted to give it a try, and then tell the driver that if they approached me again, she would cut their you-know-what off. Living in the inner-city was hard, but I had faith that God

Recognize

was going to allow me to rise above the evil that was always ever present around me.

Joann was operating under the spiritual influence of rebellion which is the sin of witchcraft. This also produced spirits of failure, hopelessness, ignorance, and perversion; while Shug was possessed by the Cocaine demon coupled with the demon of lying, cheating, and stealing. They both were sold out to Satan, and living a life that was leading them both straight to hell. Both girls came from a good background and had a mother with a beautiful spirit. Satan wanted to take both of these smart girls and make them stupid. He plotted to change the course of their lives and was successful in doing so. I believe that witchcraft was the root cause and someone in there bloodline operated in some type of an occult. They were too comfortable working as hookers. If we just learn how to call on the name of the Lord, and renounce the strongholds that are operating in our lives, God will be able to bring us out of darkness into His marvelous light.

A PRAYER FOR DELIVERANCE FROM SEXUAL SIN

Lord I am standing on Your word found in 2 Chronicles 7:14 -If my people who are called by My name shall humble themselves and pray, seek my face and turn from their wicked ways then I will hear from heaven and will forgive their sin and heal their land. Father God, I know that I am a sinner, please save me by Your grace. I confess with my mouth and believe in my heart that Your son Jesus died on the cross for my sins. I want to be a new creation in You Lord and I want to walk away and never look back on my dark past. Please teach me, lead me, and guide me into a path of righteousness. Lord, I know my sins are like scarlet, but I know that You are able to make them as white as snow, if I am obedient to Your Word. Lord I pray that You would give me direction in my new life and direction on where I should go to worship You. All have sinned and have fallen short and no one is prefect except Jesus. Lord make me more like You! In Jesus Name I Pray! Amen!

Recognize

The Flower Garden

One of my secret hiding places was the flower garden. I lived close to Sears and they had a beautiful flower garden. The garden was so beautiful that it was a little out of place being right in the heart of the Westside. I would go to the flower garden to think and to create new dance steps in my head, and to talk to God. There were only three people who knew where to find me. If all else failed, my sister Crystal, Timothy, and Michael knew my favorite spot to just go and chill. Michael was a friend of mine from the Center.

I would look at the beauty of those flowers and was reassured that there was a God. Sometimes the wind would blow and the fragrance of those flowers would fill my head with sweetness. For a brief moment all of my pain, the kind of pain I had once seen and now more clearly understood in Mary at the liquor store, was erased.

Sears had hired a guard to watch the flower garden because the kids from the neighborhood would pick the flowers or run through them. The guard made sure that no one harmed the flowers. He knew I was a regular so when I would walk slowly through the garden, or even sit on top of the wide concrete porch and just think, he simply acknowledged my presence with a slight nod of approval. The flower garden started to become my own comfort blanket.

I enjoyed watching the birds, and the squirrels enjoying nature along with me. People walking by, rushing to get to and fro. This was my get-a-way vacation. While I was in the flower garden, I could pretend that I was no longer in the ghetto.

129

Recognize

More White Walls

I started having many periods in my life where I was behind white walls. Here I am 16 and living mostly in the street, going to high school, working two part-time jobs, one at the "Y" as a dance instructor and two, braiding hair when possible; and, still trying to keep in sync with the rest of the world. Somehow, I was making it.

By now, I was back at my mother's place. I tried to stay out of her way by leaving out of the house early in the morning and returning when it was time to go to bed. I started to enjoy working with the girls at the Center because I started to see improvement in their behavior and I noticed how they were beginning to take pride in being apart of the YMCA drill and dance teams. The only thing that was missing is that they didn't have any uniforms or anything decent to practice in. Some of them had on dirty clothes and smelly underwear, and others had on clothes two sizes to small for them to move in, so I decided to take a bus downtown to a place where the high school bought their uniforms and made a deal with the owner to get seventy red body suits and matching tights. This was a big sacrifice for me to spend all of my money on the girls, but it was worth seeing the smiles on their faces when I handed them their own leotard. I wanted them to feel like dancers. I wanted them to start taking more pride in themselves and their things. They all came from low-income families and couldn't afford to buy dance attire. So, I took one of my paychecks (even though I needed it for myself), went to my gym teacher at school and asked her where did she get the pom-pom uniforms. I told her that I wanted to get some inexpensive

Recognize

dance stuff for my class at the Center. After a few phone calls and getting a few donations from the Center, I was able to get seventy outfits for my dance class. It was a happy day.

The girls were so excited. For the first time in their lives, some of them felt pretty and a little special. This is what I was striving for. Their minds were too often occupied with thoughts about fighting. I wanted to teach them that there were other things in life besides fighting. I was so determined to get them out of the bad habit of fighting that I came up with a few new rules: anyone caught name-calling would be suspended from the center for one day; anyone caught starting a fight with that 'he said, she said' stuff, would be suspended from the Center for two days; anyone caught fighting would be suspended for three days and may not be able to participate in the inter-city dance competition.

This particular winter evening, I let the girls go home early. I was tired and they had worked really hard for our upcoming event. I was heading to the bathroom and heard a lot of noise and name-calling. By the time I made it to the first floor, there were about fifteen girls entangled with hands full of hair, book bags being tossed about, and general chaos. It took about 10 of us to pull these young people apart.

Timothy told me to handle the situation and to see him in his office when I was finished. I was not a happy camper. I had just told Timothy that my girls were finally starting to act like ladies and that my class was under control. I told all involved in the fight to meet me in the gym room and for everyone else to go home. As I talked to the girls to hear all 15 sides of their stories, I let them know that I was very disappointed in them and that I had no other choice than to suspend them all. The Director of the Center came in to speak to the girls and told them that they acted worse than the boys, and that they were to go home and not come back for a week. He also added that if he had to deal with any of them in the future, they would be barred from the Center forever. This reprimand was traumatic for me as well. I remembered how I started with these girls–how my initial start on the job was very shaky–but now experience had made me a veteran. I had worked for Timothy for 3 years all-year round. In the summer I would work a full eight hour day, and in the winter I would work part-time after school. I had spent a lot of time with these girls, teaching hygiene, the importance of a good education, avoiding single parenthood, and non-violence. I had taught that fighting wasn't the appropriate way for a young girl to express herself.

My rules were always coupled with love and understanding. I knew that many of these girls' parents couldn't afford to get workout and dance attire–that is why I spent my entire paycheck on getting everything that these girls needed even though still in need myself. After hearing all sides of everyone's story, I decided to suspend about eleven girls. They were not allowed to attend any of the Center activities for three days. I believe that this decision hurt me as much as it did them. I know that they needed the activities at the 'Y', but they also needed to know that there was a price for their actions.

Timothy stated that he was proud of the way I handled the girls. He expressed that he felt I was always too easy on them and that they would never learn if I didn't enforce my rules. "How do you feel about sending the girls home?" Timothy asked. "Well, I didn't want to do it, but you're right

Recognize

in that they need to learn how to follow rules." "It's late, do you need a ride home?" Timothy asked. "No, I'll walk. I have a few things I need to meditate on and walking home will give me the time to do just that." Timothy commented with some concern, "After all of the commotion that has taken place today, I figured you could use a ride home." "I'll be all right," I said with confidence.

I put my workout clothes into my bookbag and headed home. Half-way home, I noticed a crowd of people headed in my direction. Some on bikes, others on skates, and many on foot. By the time I got mid-way between a nearby department store parking garage and home, a young man on a ten speed bike rode in front of me to block my path. He then began to ride around me in circles keeping me from moving forward. He made several revolutions around me. This was his way of keeping me from getting closer to home and to allow the crowd of people to catch up with me.

I really didn't know what was going on until I noticed that several of the people in the crowd were from my dance class. I was really glad to see them and wanted to know what they were doing outside so late. The next thing I knew, I was surrounded by more than 60 people all from a nearby housing project. Many were friends and family members of the girls from my dance class. I didn't think anything serious would take place. After all, I had not only taught these girls vital life skills, but I was also supplying them with clothing and other items "out of pocket."

A large woman got in my face and pointed at me and said, "Is this the B-----?" "Yeah," came from the crowd. She began to call me all kinds of foul names and told me that tonight was my last night on earth. I was a little nervous, but a mysterious calm came over me at the same time. I felt that if I could maybe talk to the crowd, I could defuse the situation. With so many adults in the gathering, certainly I could make sense to them. "Everyone, please calm down," I said with confidence. "I did not suspend your daughters and sisters to be mean. I love these girls. I'm the one who bought the clothes they are currently wearing. I have gone out of my way for these girls. I am not out to hurt them, but to help them. I have spent much time teaching them non-violence. I don't plan to be apart of any violent act tonight. After three days, all the girls are welcome back into the Center. This is just one way of teaching the girls right from wrong."

"This little skinny b----- think she's running thangs," someone said from the crowd. "We should 'whup' her a-- and leave her here for dead," someone else shouted. At this point I realized that I was in a very hostile situation. Good biblical language would have recorded, "O woe is me." These girls didn't know anything but violence because they came from a community of violent people.

It wasn't always this way in our neighborhood according to my historical recollections. But the man I knew as the father of non-violence had triggered one of the worst riots of the century right down the street. He had died violently even though he lived non-violently and preached the same. Was I going to duplicate the fate of Martin Luther King, Jr.?

Things were turning for the worst. The next thing I knew, a young man on a ten speed bike road up behind me and held a 35 mm gun to my head, and asked the crowd if he should blow my brains out. Someone from the crowd said, "Naw

Recognize

man, don't kill her. We don't want her dead, we just want her to know not to f--k with our people." At this point he turned the gun around and used the handle to bust a hole in my head. He hit me in the head so hard with that gun that blood came streaming down my head and all over the back of my coat. I held my right eye first because it felt like my eye had popped out of my head, and then I grabbed the back of my head to slow the bleeding down. I then fell to the ground in a half conscious state.

I could feel people kicking me, stumping me, and riding over me with their bikes. I remember thinking that this is what hell must feel like.

I heard gun shots from afar, and someone picking me up from the ground. It was Ricky, Shug's man. He "ran" the streets and nothing went on in his area without him knowing about it. When he saw what was going on, he took his gun and shot it in the air to clear the area. When he saw that it was me being attacked, he took action. By this time, Timothy was pulling up. He said that he didn't feel right after I left the Center. He said he didn't know what was up, but he felt like he needed to double check to see if I made it home okay. My mother called the police and I was rushed to a nearby hospital for immediate attention. I was diagnosed with a concussion and had to have many stitches in my head.

They pinned me to a table face down so that I had the hole exposed. Then I felt the worst pain in life. They stuck a long needle in my head to deaden it so that they could stitch me up. After two to three shots to my head, they shaved off half of my hair from the ears down. I was sad, mad, sick, and in a lot of pain. I did not want to continue living this life. I would always think of Jesus when I was in this kind of pain, not physical pain, but emotional pain. How could those girls let me go down like that after all I'd done for them? I guess this is how Christ felt when he went down on Calvary. People would always tell me that I did too much for others with little return. But I can only do what God tells me to do and that is treating others the way I would want to be treated. Where was my error?

I was sent home with a mummy wrapped head, pain pills, and instructions to stay in bed for the next two days. The doctor told my mom that I was not to overwork myself. I was very dizzy anytime I tried to stand to my feet. The doctor stressed that I shouldn't do any stairs for awhile to avoid falling.

The next day after the news got out, there were riots everywhere. Fights broke out at the Center, near my school and over at the housing projects where most of the offenders lived. I had to have police protection for a while as bricks were flying through my mom's window every other day. The Center was closed down for several weeks, and I wasn't able to go to school until the violence calmed down.

Months later, I had to appear in court with the offender. Our first court appearance was so out of control and there were so many people attending that the judge sent everyone home and arranged for the next court hearing to be closed to the public. After all of the preliminaries, the offender was charged with battery and received one year probation. As we left the court room, he whispered to me that if he had to do it all over again, he would have killed me. My brother said to him, "You better be glad I wasn't out there that night," and

Recognize

hit the guy in the face. The police were right there to break up the fight. Things never did get back to normal.

One day at the Center as I spent another day in Timothy's office, he said, "You know you can't spend everyday in my office doing nothing. You have to start your dance class back up." I responded, "I don't want to be bothered with those hoodlums anymore. You can fire me, send me home or whatever you want to do, at this point I don't care. Life sucks anyway." Timothy didn't have much to say. He knew I needed this little piece of a job, and he also knew I needed time to recover from everything that had happened to me. I had to wear a hat for a while because half of my head was bald, and I felt like I didn't owe anyone anything.

I didn't want to hear another one of Timothy's stories about how these kids don't know nothing about love, peace and joy or how they needed me. What about me? What about what I'm going through, what about me and my bald head? What about all the money I spent on those ungrateful kids? I hated everything around me and I couldn't help the way I felt. I wanted to love like Jesus but I couldn't find or feel the love. The girls would meet me at the door of the Center every evening and ask me if we were going to have dance class today, and I would say no without looking at them and would tell them to go home.

One evening while I was in Timothy's office doing my homework (while on the clock), Timothy called me into the hallway and said there were some people there to see me. Was it a local newspaper, the police, more gang members? I was wondering who could it be. I didn't want any surprises so I yelled, "Who is it?" He said come and see. As I stepped into the hallway, I saw many of the same faces I saw the night my head got busted. They had cakes, pies and sympathy cards that they wanted to share with me. Some of the smaller kids ran up to me and wrapped themselves around my legs and told me how much they missed me. One mother begged me to please start up my dance class again. She told me that all three of her daughters were doing much better in school and that they helped her more around the house just to get to my dance class. Another mother apologized for what had happened to me and that they really wanted me to start the class up again.

"Why should I?" I asked. "Our kids love you, they need you, they miss you, and we know what happened to you wasn't right, and we all plan to support you and all of your rules," they replied. "We baked you some cakes and pies and hope you can forgive us for everything." I felt good that they would go through such trouble to show their appreciation for my hard work, but I wasn't taking any chances on eating anything that they had baked for me.

Starting up the class again was something I would at least think about. I asked them to take the goodies downstairs so everyone could partake. I would not have been able to take all of that stuff home, and plus I was still trying to figure out if they could be trusted. I knew that something evil was always around trying to take me off of this earth, but I couldn't figure out why. I was just a young girl trying to make it. Someone who was aware that there is always someone else worse off than me. I tried never to stay in a low place and wanted to simply show others how to come out from the low places. I wish I knew how to plead the "Blood

Recognize

of Jesus" during this time because just maybe Satan wouldn't have been able to get so close.

I now recognize that Satan was trying to sentence me to an early death. He wanted me to stay in darkness because He knew I would be in the army of the Lord. Now that I'm aware of his little plot, I plan to fight with all that is within me with the help and guidance of the Holy Spirit. I had to learn how to love unconditionally and give to a need out of my own needs. God was teaching me how to walk by faith and not by situations and conditions. I'm determined to walk with the Lord and can't no devil in hell stop me. If you've ever been hurt by anyone, you need healing and deliverance.

A PRAYER OF FORGIVENESS
AND HEALING

Father God, I pray for everyone who has hurt me, and who has spitefully used me. Lord restore me and teach me how to love with Your love. Give me the strength to forgive my enemies, and to love those who hate me. I thank you for every test and trial because I know that they come to make me strong. Lord I praise and thank You that You will not put more on me than I can bear. Please keep me in Your will, and in Your perfect peace. Touch my emotions, and heal me the way that only You can do, In Jesus Mighty Name! Amen!

Recognize

Meet Mike and Steve

What else is going on at the 'Y'? One thing I often thought about was how many guys are betting that they would be the first to sleep with me. See, one of the things that boys would do in my neighborhood was add up the number of girls they had slept with, and put bets out on who would sleep with whom first. I remember a time when my brothers thought I was asleep as we all slept in the same room. They were talking about who would get Denise first. She was a friend of mine and was built like a grown woman. The way that they would prove that they had 'hit it' which was a street term for 'slept with' was by keeping the smell of her vagina on their finger. I had a lot of insight on the games that boys played because I would ease drop on my brothers' conversations.

Mike and I were good friends. He would sneak me in his house at night when his parents were asleep and never tried to hit it. I really started to like Mike, but didn't want to have sex or anything as I wasn't sure if he was apart of the boys club. After all, I didn't want to be apart of a bet. One day while I was at Mike's house, he said, "You know you are on the bet list." "What bet list?" I asked but really already knew what he was referring to. "The 'who's going to sleep with Toni first' bet list." "Are you apart of the bet?" I asked. "No, I'm just letting you know what's up." "Cool, thanks for looking out," I said. Mike and I attended two different schools. I transferred to a new school (Collins) on the Westside while he remained at our old school. But he and I would see each other over at the YMCA all the time. I was there working with my dance class while he played ball.

Recognize

Timothy wanted to know if I was dating Mike, I told him not really. I just get to stay at his house every now and then. "Well be careful. If you need to get some pills I have a doctor friend I could put you in contact with." "No thanks, I don't plan to give it up. I don't want any of the boys to win the bet." "Oh, so you know about the bet?" he said. "Yes, I know all about the bet." Timothy smiled and walked away as if he was pleased that I was on top of my game.

"Hello Ms. 'T,' Steve said. "Hi," I said. "Is that the best you can do?" Steve asked. "What do you want me to say?" "Well I was just hoping I could get a minute of your time to get to know you a little better," he said. The only thing I could think about is if he was apart of the bet. He was good looking, athletic, but from what I could remember he had a girlfriend that played ball for Marshall High School and I wasn't in the mood for dealing with those gangster girls. Many of them had more muscle than the guys. I told Steve that I was busy and that I would talk to him later.

At the 'Y,' no one had best friends. We were all friends. Sometimes I would watch the guys play ball and other times, they would watch me teach my dance class. The 'Y' was the hang out place, the fighting place, the skating place, and the pick-up place. It was just the place to be.

Mike and I were like brother and sister and I really started to like him because it appeared that he was risking his life to sneak me in his house so often, until one day when his father came in his room to wake him up for school. I was hiding under the covers at the time, and his father said, "Get up Mike, and you too Toni." His father knew all along that Michael had been sneaking me in his room. One day I had the nerve to ask Mike's father how did he know that I was in Mike's room, and he said, "A real man always knows what is going on in his house."

I left Mike behind because I had to be at a student counsel meeting and plus I had a further distance to walk than him. On my way to school I ran into Steve. "Are you and Mike dating?" he asked. "No, we are just friends. Why?" "Well, I just wanted you to know that if Mike was your man then he wouldn't have a bet out on you. If you were my woman, I wouldn't let anyone bet on you." "You are lying, Mike doesn't have a bet out on me!" "How much you want to bet? After school meet me at the 'Y' and I will prove to you that Mike has a bet out on you." I just kept walking and didn't want to believe that Mike would be apart of such a stupid game.

Steve told me to stand behind a door while he called Mike up the stairs. "What's up Steve?" "Did you hit it yet?" "No! Give me a little more time," Mike said. "Man, we have a lot of dough on the table, you are taking too long." Mike said, "I'm working on it, just give me a little more time." I stepped from behind the door and looked at Michael with tears in my eyes. I couldn't believe that he was apart of a stupid bet. He looked like he had just seen a ghost, and Steve had a huge smile on his face. I just walked away.

I started spending more time outside because I didn't want to be with Mike anymore. I didn't trust him. One day I was balled up outside trying to keep warm and saw Steve's mother driving by. She stopped and asked me why don't I go inside and get warm. I told her that I couldn't do that. She told me to get in and took me to her house. Mrs. Washington was a church mother. She had eight boys and a husband who had just committed suicide two years prior. The rumor had it that her husband used to hear the voices of demons, and one of them told him to kill himself.

When we walked in her house it was so clean, and I could smell that something great was cooking on the stove. She ran her house like a military camp. She only had five of her boys at home, Steve being one of them, as the others were grown and gone. They were all looking at me like I was a piece of steak and they were hungry dogs that hadn't eaten in weeks. Mrs. Washington said, "What the f--k y'all looking at, get y'all butts somewhere and sit down. You act like you never seen a girl before." For a church lady, she sure could curse.

She told me that I could sleep on the couch. We were on the first floor of a two flat she owned. Some of her boys slept upstairs and some in the basement. Mrs. Washington and her youngest spoiled baby boy slept on the first floor. Her baby boy was two years older than me, and Steve was one year older than him. She babied her youngest son, because from what I understood, he witnessed his father putting a bullet through his head.

The couch was comfortable and the house was quiet. I slept pretty well for a change. As I got up to get ready for school, I saw Steve outside with his two dogs. I forgot that they had dogs. The house was so clean and did not smell like dogs lived there. Steve had two Doberman Pinchers, one red and the other one was black. These dogs were big and treacherous. I was told that the dogs once belonged to Steve's father, and the only other person that these dogs would listen to was Steve. I waited until he took the dogs back into the basement from the back of the house before I left out the front door to go to school. I didn't want him using me for any type of example or incorporating me into his morning routine along with the dogs.

Mrs. Washington's bedroom door was closed, so I just yelled out, "Goodbye Mrs. Washington, I'm on my way to school now. Thanks for letting me spend the night." She yelled back, "No problem, you are welcome anytime." Off to school I went. By the time I made it to the 'Y' the guys were surrounding Steve and it looked like they were paying Steve off. From what Mike told me, Steve told everyone that I spent the night with him and he "hit it." He was getting and giving out 'Hi Five's' and getting paid by all the boys. I was really pissed off so to make Steve look like a fool for lying, I kissed Michael in front of all the guys and told them that Mike was the one who "hit it" not Steve, and that Mike won the bet, not Steve. Steve had to give up all the cash. Mike took it and wanted to know if I wanted the money. I told him to keep it.

One Saturday evening I wanted to just chill, so I went to Mrs. Washington's house. Steve was at the 'Y' and I knew that Mrs. Washington was probably at home working on her Sunday dinner and getting prepared for Sunday school. "Come on in baby, I was just leaving out to do some grocery shopping. Make yourself at home." "Where are the dogs?" I asked. "They are in the basement. You don't ever have to worry about them being in my house. Even when my husband was alive, they were not allowed in my house." Cool, I was fine with that. I just didn't want to be their next meal.

Recognize

Later on, Steve came home and went straight downstairs to shower. I didn't think he saw me sitting on the couch, which was a plus for me. But after about ten minutes he was standing in the living room with both dogs launching out at me as he held them back by their chains. He said, "What do you think these dogs would do if I let them go?" I wasn't in the mood to play with Steve and his killer dogs. So, I just asked him to put them away because I was afraid of them. He said that I had to come with him down into the basement, or he would let both dogs go, and that he wouldn't be responsible for what they'd do to me. I sat and thought for a moment, took a good look around me, and figured that I could out run the dogs and make it out of the back door. I stood up slowly and took off for the back door. Steve told the dogs to get me, and those dogs were on me so fast I could feel their breath on my leg through my pants. "Sit, sit!" Steve said. They pinned me between the back door and them. They both were looking at me with all their teeth showing and with the most vicious faces I had ever seen on a dog. Steve said, "That was a stupid move. Now where are you going to go?" My heart was beating so fast and my head was hurting so bad that I thought I was going to faint. "Your mother told me that these dogs are not allowed upstairs in her house," I said. "Yeah, but my mother isn't here, is she?"

He told me that if I didn't come to the basement with him, that he would let his dogs eat me alive. "I will tell my mother and the police that you were roaming around the house and went into the basement, and the rest was history." I walked down to the basement with him thinking all the while that this is the day that I'm going to be raped. I prayed to God under my breath, "LORD, please don't let him rape me. I don't want this to happen this way. HELP ME

LORD! HELP ME LORD!" I was feeling for my knife and remembered that it was in my book bag.

Steve let his dogs roam the basement just in case I had an escape plan. I asked him to put the dogs in their cages but he wouldn't. All of a sudden, we heard footsteps coming down into the basement. Steve said "Shhhh you better not say a word." He went to the stairs but it was only his younger brother. "What's Toni doing down here?" he asked. "Don't worry about it, just look out for Mama." Steve got undressed and made me get undressed and was trying to help me by snatching some of the buttons off my blouse. As he wrestled me to the bed, he got on top of me and was trying to penetrate me. I told him that he was hurting me and I wanted him to get up. There were more footsteps. Steve's brother yelled, "It's Mom, it's Mom. Hide Toni, she's coming down here." Steve made me get under the bed and both he and his brother sat on the bed hoping that their mother would go back upstairs. I was making noise, and both Steve and his brother began to bounce up and down on the small twin bed to make their Mother think that the noise coming from the bed was them and not me.

Now, my hair got caught by a hanging spring from under the bed, and then one of the shoes began to move. All of the shoes under the bed were pretty large. But, come to find out, it wasn't a shoe, it was a rat. I tried to free my hair and move away from the rat while trying to keep the two boys from smashing me under the bed. I started kicking and moaning more as I didn't want the rat to bite me in the face. The rat was just as afraid as I was, or so it appeared. It sounded like Mrs. Washington was heading back up the stairs. I thought it was strange that she didn't ask if I had left. All I could

Recognize

think was that I was living a life of hell and wanted it to end. They finally let me up and told me to go out the back door. I pleaded with Steve not to let those dogs get me. He held the dogs until I got out of the basement and into the alley (another day in the streets).

As I walked through the alley to the main street I could feel an uncomfortable feeling between my legs. I felt dirty and ugly. I wanted to tell somebody about what had happened, but I also didn't want anyone to know. I was taken advantage of and could have been totally violated, but I was violated enough. I guessed something like this was bound to happen since I was always in the streets. I was always hanging out with the hookers, and sleeping anywhere I could get a halfway decent nap. A girl like me should feel lucky that worse didn't happen. Isn't that what people would think? Anyway, who could I tell? Timothy would probably snap. My brothers would start a holy Westside war. Some people may say, "That's what she get," and telling the Magic Man was out of the question. Steve would be found in the street dead as a dog, and he really didn't deserve to die. Besides, his mother was still dealing with the loss of her husband. One thing for sure, one violent act of defiance can lead to another. Do I keep the cycle of drama going or do I stop it? I went to the flower garden to think it over.

I decided to drop it, and make sure not to put myself into harms way again. The next day as I entered the 'Y', who do I run into? - Steve and his butch looking girlfriend standing right in the doorway mopping each other's faces with their tongues. He looked at me with a smirk on his face while his tongue was still partially in his girl's mouth, and I looked at him in disgust, and kept toward the gym room. I started to make a big scene, but I fought the feeling.

Later he came to my dance class and wanted to know if we could talk. I told him to stay away from me before all hell broke loose, and I made sure to stay away from him. We both worked at the 'Y' for another year or so, and we both tried to act normal around each other, whatever normal was.

Satan's plot against me was always in the atmosphere, but I am grateful that God kept His arms around me, and I don't plan to let God's protection go to waste. I had to live by faith like never before. I had to believe that God would keep me and never let any evil plot prevail against me. The attacks were heavy, but victory was my portion.

Recognize

A PRAYER FOR EVERY
RAPE VICTIM

Father God help me to forgive those who have trespassed against me. Send Your ministering angel to restore me and to protect me. I will not walk in fear because You did not give me a spirit of fear, but that of love, power and a sound mind. I will live my life by faith, prayer, and trust that You are the author of my life. Help me to be whole again. Help me to trust again, and help me to remove any anger and pain that would try to come and take my joy away. I love You God, and I ask You to be my protector. I bind up every unclean and wicked spirit that would come and try to eat up my flesh. Cover me with your blood and keep me out of harms way, in Jesus' Name I pray! AMEN!

Meet My First College Friends

Somehow, I made it out of High School. I did okay on the S.A.T. test, but my reading scores were so low that it was hard for me to get into any college. My college counselor came up with an idea that would address this problem, along with a serious commitment from me. He was able to get me into Northeastern with English as a second language. I really wanted to go away to college thinking that at least I would have a steady place to lay my head. Unfortunately, I didn't have the finances, the grade scores, or the support from any family member to pull this idea off.

College, what could life have in store for me now? My first day on campus was with my student counselor. He explained to me how important it was for me to do my best in school as I was kind of on some type of academic probation. The group that I was assigned to was a group of foreigners from all over the world who could barely speak English. I was still trying to figure out if I liked them as they were in school for free and getting everything handed to them on a silver platter. They all were looking at me as if I was the foreigner. Maybe I was because I was the only one from this country that had to get a student loan, along with my student aid just to attend the school. I asked my counselor if he could work something out where I could come here for free since I was in a foreigner exchange program.

Needless to say I had to foot my college bill the best way I could. I was still working at the 'Y', but it was no longer bringing in the type of cash I needed. Something had to change. One day a Chinese girl tried to ask me my name. It

153

Recognize

took me about 5 minutes to figure out what she was trying to ask me. After a few weeks I made friends with a Chinese girl, an Indian girl, and a white girl. I had never had anything but black friends so this was a new adventure. We would walk the halls and eat lunch together. People started calling us the United Nations.

One day we all decided to experience each other's life. We wanted to see what it was like to live like a Chinese, or Indian, or White or Black. It was my idea, but after I thought about it I didn't think it was such a good idea because I didn't want to bring those prima donna's to the Westside of Chicago. I was a little concerned for their safety. We all started out at the Chinese girl's house. Her mom and dad were very friendly. We had Chinese food and we got to eat on the floor. That was pretty cool. Next we went over to the Indian girl's house. They looked like they had money. Her mom had on fourteen maybe twenty-two karat gold jewelry (the real stuff), and her dad drove a really nice car, but they didn't have much living room and dining room furniture. I really didn't like the smell in the house and my Indian friend had to explain to us that that was the smell of curry, a seasoning that her mother used in most of her food. We sat at the kitchen table to eat, but I couldn't take that smell, so I just passed. We talked about arranged marriages and how it was a disgrace to the family if an Indian girl had sex before marriage. The Chinese girl said that that's how things were back home, but she wanted to marry whomever she liked. This is one of the reasons the girls liked being in America. I was thinking to myself that in America, from where I grew up, the girls were giving it up at thirteen and weren't thinking about disgracing nobody. They were doing what they learned from their mama's. As far as marriage, I didn't see much of that. Most of my friends didn't know who their daddies were, or in most cases, the people I knew all were sisters and bothers who had different fathers. At this point I didn't have a lot to say. I just sat and listened. I didn't want to distort their perfect image of America. My grandmother taught me that if you don't have anything good to say, don't say anything at all.

About a month later it was my turn to entertain the girls. I knew my mother wouldn't like the idea of bringing these girls to her house for dinner. I could barely get anything to eat myself, so I decided to take them to a church gospel concert, the kind where the choir would rock the house. They all believed in God, I thought, and it would be a pretty cool "Black" experience. I felt like nobody knew how to raise the church roof like a black choir. The white girl had a car and she picked us all up and we went to a church on the Westside. The girls were too naive to be afraid. They just wanted a black experience. As I walked in with these girls, people were looking as if I had just brought in the President. The girls were excited because they were the center of attraction. We took our seats and I fielded what appeared to be a thousand questions about the black church, the choir, etc. I couldn't wait to see their faces when the choir got into their groove.

The choir was pretty calm during the first two songs, now it was time for them to sing "JOY". Before the choir could get the first word out, the entire church was on their feet, except us, as the girls didn't know if it was okay to stand and clap. They just sat there looking around as if they were on the moon for the first time. The choir sang the chorus of the song, then broke it down by Sopranos, Altos and Tenors. They sang that song so hard and so loud that they raised the

Recognize

roof off the sucker. People were singing, clapping, running, and shouting. The girls were just sitting there in shock. As I looked at their faces, I couldn't help myself. I was tickled and couldn't stop laughing.

We left before the concert was over, and went to get a bite to eat. The Chinese and Indian girls both had curfews. The white girl and I could pretty much do what we wanted. I asked Kathy (the white girl) how did she end up in a foreign program. I thought all white people were smart. I had this impression because a lot of my teachers were white. She told me that she was a very sickly kid and missed a lot of school. I told her that I missed a lot of school also, but didn't go into a lot of details.

Meet My Baby's Daddy

One day the United Nations and I were sitting in the lunchroom cafeteria and this guy walked over with his guitar and wanted to sit with us. We all just looked at each other and wanted to know what was up. He looked at me and asked me my name and the other girls just laughed, "Toni," I said. "Toni! That's a boy's name." "What is your name?" I asked. "Sandy," he said. "Sandy, that's a girl's name," I said. "Well we got a match, one girl and one boy," he said, and the girls laughed. "What can we do for you?" I asked. "You can meet me for breakfast tomorrow morning," he said. "How do you know that I even do breakfast?" I asked. "Because I see you in the morning everyday trying to get your nickels together to buy breakfast, and tomorrow it will be my treat." "I'm cool with that," I said.

We all had to get to class, and I didn't need to be late for my dance class as I was the only one who didn't have any real professional dance background and the teacher was really hard on me. All the other girls were from this school of ballet and that school of ballet, and they all had their mothers fussing over them all the time. The teacher would give out dance commands and I was trying to keep up as best I could and was trying not to crash into any of my classmates.

This cute black girl from France was a very good dancer and wanted to help me. After all, we were the only two black girls in the class. You're from France?" I asked. "Yes, you act surprised," she said. "I am surprised. I didn't know black people lived in France." "Yes, Totee, there are lots of us." She had a pretty cool accent. She didn't call me Toni. She

Recognize

called me Totee. She worked with me for months until I started to feel like a real dancer.

Sandy was waiting for me in the cafeteria. He told me to get whatever I wanted and he would foot the bill. We started spending every morning together discussing life. He wanted to know why all of my friends were foreigners and he wanted to know where I lived. He spent much of his time asking me a bunch of questions. While on the other hand, I wanted to know who was that cute tall girl he's with all the time. "Is she your girlfriend?" I asked. He told me that she was in his music class and that she was a great drummer.

It was now time for my white friend Kathy to entertain the group. She asked her parents if she could have a sleepover. Her parents gave her permission, but the Chinese and Indian girls could not stay out overnight, so it was just Kathy and I. Kathy had a big beautiful house. It was out in the burbs somewhere. The block was beautiful, peaceful, and the snow on the houses looked like something you would see on a Christmas card. I really liked Kathy. I started feeling like the work that Martin Luther King Jr. did paid off because I hadn't experienced any racism in all of my twenty years of living. All my white teachers were nice for the most part, and Kathy was really, really cool, and she didn't seem to have any hang ups about me being black.

As I walked in the front door, I noticed a cross on the mantel that was positioned upside down. I figured it must have fallen and someone didn't have the patience to put it back in its upright position. I fixed it and followed Kathy down the stairs to her finished plush basement. We ate popcorn, drank pop, watched movies and played with her small and cute little doggy. I hadn't had this much fun in, well never. You will learn more about their other dog later.

We both started to get sleepy. She took me upstairs and showed me to the guest room. Her mom and dad were still out. It had to be about 12 midnight. I looked around the room and waited for Kathy to leave out. I started jumping up and down on the bed, smelling the fresh sheets, and just couldn't believe I was in such a nice house. I was ready to be adopted and be Kathy's black sister. As soon as my head hit the pillow I was out.

Time passed and I was awakened by an arguing man and woman who had a vicious dog on a leash: a black Doberman. "Kathy, what is this nigger doing in my house?" "This is Toni from school. I told you that she was coming!" Kathy said. "Yeah, but you didn't tell me that she was a nigger," her dad said. "GET THIS NIGGER OUT OF MY HOUSE RIGHT NOW!!!" he said. While the shouting was yet going on, and the mother taking the glass that I drank out of and smashing it against the fireplace, I was getting my things as fast as I could. The father was helping out by tossing my things out into the streets. I could here the mother saying, "I can't believe that we have a nigger in our house." I finished putting my clothes on as I stood in the snow. I didn't know where I was or which way to go. I was afraid that they would call some of their white friends to catch me on the block and lynch me.

I walked until I found a pay phone. I couldn't think of anyone else to call so I called my mother. I explained to her my situation, and she was pissed. "What the f--k you want me to do? I don't have a car. I don't have any money. Besides,

Recognize

it's 3 o'clock in the morning," she said. I held back my tears and said, "All I need you to do is pay for a cab to come and get me and I will find a way to pay you back." "How in the hell am I going to call a cab and you don't even know where in the f--k you are?" she said. I told my mother that I would figure something out and hung up. After walking for about two hours, I was able to flag down a cab. The cab took me home and waited until I ran into the house to get money from my mother. She tossed me the money and I promised to pay her back. I ran out to the cab, paid him and slept at the foot of my sister's bed. I didn't even bother to take my clothes off. Besides they may have been frozen onto my skin.

The next day at breakfast I told Sandy what happened. He asked me why I didn't call him. I told him that I didn't have his number. He gave me a work number. Sandy worked at the Hyatt as a waiter. He said he could get me a job there if I needed a job. I told him that I really needed a job and a place to stay. He promised that he would work it out where I could work as a cashier and still go to school during the day. Since we both worked at the Hyatt he would see to it that I got back and forth to work.

One day I saw Kathy and the other girls in the cafeteria. She walked over to me to explain her parent's behavior. She told me that her parents were Ku Klux Klan and that she was raised to hate blacks, but she had never met any black people until she met me and really liked me. "Why didn't you tell your parents that I was black?" I asked. She said that she didn't think it would matter. She said, "Toni, you got to believe me. I don't think like my parents. They hate people for no reason, but I don't. I really like being your friend," she said. "Friends don't put their friends in harms way. I would never put you in a situation where you could get hurt," I said as I walked away. She said, "Toni, it's not my fault, it's not my fault!" I just wanted to be left alone. I needed time to work out my life and didn't need dogs, whites, or anything else chasing me.

Sandy wasn't at our usual breakfast hangout so I went to the music area looking for him. I saw him and the drummer girl all hugged up so I just turned around and went to my class a little early. I needed the practice anyway. Sandy stopped by my mother's house after seeing our building on the 10 o'clock news. The building was on fire and the firemen were on strike. Five people died in the fire and we all were burned out. The only things I had to my name were my books, dance and workout stuff. This was my night off and I really wanted to get a good night's rest as our production was the next day. Sandy honked his horn and asked me to get in. "What are you doing?" he asked. "Just sitting in front of a burned up building wondering where I'm going to go." I said. "Where is everyone else?" he asked. "Here and there," I said. "Hey, where have you been the last few weeks? I've been missing you," he said. "Well I didn't want to get in the way of you and the drummer girl. I saw you two hugged up in the music room," I said. But he didn't have any comments. He made arrangements for me to stay at the Hyatt for a few days, and was going to check to see if I could stay with his mom for a while.

"I thought you had your own place. Why do I need to stay with your mom? Do you think I'm going to cramp your style? You can tell your women that I'm just your sister. I'm not trying to get with you. I just need a place to stay, so I don't get kicked out of school. I'm on academic probation."

Recognize

"I just need to work a few things out before you can stay with me," he said. His mother lived in a high-rise building with a doorman on the North side of Chicago. The place was okay, but looked like it needed a good cleaning. His mom wasn't there when we walked in. He said, "I'll be back. Just chill here for a while and I'll come and get you." I didn't hear from Sandy for two days and his mother never showed up. I didn't feel comfortable being at someone's apartment whom I had never met. This just didn't feel right.

It was an early Saturday morning, and I could hear someone trying to get in with a key. I was hoping that it was Sandy, but it was a lady who looked like she rode a motorcycle. She had on all black leather, a cheap wig, and had a horrible scar across her face where she must have had stitches. She was drunk, tall, ugly, and surprised to see me. I sat up in the bed and just looked at her. She said, "Who in the f--k are you!?" "I'm Sandy's friend." "Well you got to get the f--k out of here, because I'm not in the mood for company." I gathered my things and left. I called Sandy to see if I could meet him at the Hyatt for a little while.

One Friday night Sandy asked me if I wanted to spend the night with him. I wasn't sure if he meant at the Hyatt, at his mom's or at his "real" home, but never-the-less, I didn't have a whole lot of options and said yes. He took me to a really nice apartment with three large bedrooms on the North side of Chicago. The place had beautiful hardwood floors, a sun room with beautiful plants and all of the rooms were color prefect, everything matched like out of House and Garden magazine. I almost felt like a woman lived there. "Do you live here by yourself?" I asked. "Yes. What do you think, a man can't have taste?" "No, I didn't say that, you did. This place is beautiful, why are you just now letting me come over and you know my situation?" "Well, you're here now, that's all that matters." We laid across the bed and ate our hotdogs and french fries that we picked up before and watched a little TV. I really liked his apartment, but it felt like this wasn't his place or something like that. Something just wasn't adding up.

He asked me if I wanted to take a shower, but I thought he just wanted me to be fresh for a little sex, so I told him that I would take a shower in the morning, so he took one instead. While he was in the shower, I got up and peeked in the bedroom closet, and all I saw were his suits all lined up. I still wasn't satisfied, so I went into the closets in the other bedrooms and just like I suspected, it was full of women's clothes and shoes. I put my foot in one of the pumps and it had to be two to three sizes too large, so I figured she had to be a pretty large woman. I made my way back to the main bedroom and just laid there as if I had been there all along.

What do I say? I didn't even have the right to snoop, but on the other hand, he didn't have the right to lie to me. I found that I couldn't sleep. Who is she? What does she do? Is she rich? Is she out of town and if so when will she be back? What would happen if she came home in the middle of the night and found me here? My feeling of relaxation went out the window, and all of a sudden I didn't have a whole lot of conversation and Sandy noticed it. I just really wanted this vagabond lifestyle that I had to end. I had to tell myself to relax and just go to sleep.

I don't know how long I was asleep when Sandy yelled, "Toni, Toni, get up! Get up!" I thought the house was on

Recognize

fire, so I roamed around half-sleep saying, "What! What! What!" I really forgot where I was. Things were moving so fast that I couldn't remember a whole lot. Sandy grabbed most of my things and pushed me out the back door. I'm standing on his back porch with my clothes in my hand and wondering, "What the hell is going on." Seconds later, he comes out the back door with his car key telling me to meet him in the car. I knew what had happened, the woman with the big feet made it home sooner than he thought, and I was caught in the middle of it all.

I had to be sitting in the car for about an hour, and when I looked up I saw Sandy running toward the car and a very tall woman after him with a stick or bat or something in her hand. He jumped in the car and took off with me in it without any explanation. We just rode around for a while in silence, and then we finally went to the Hyatt and got a room for the remainder of the night. I had so many questions, many more comments, but I kept them to myself. After all he was the only person who was trying to help me out or so I thought.

The next morning, I asked him did he get my school bag, because I noticed that it wasn't in the car. We looked and looked and finally decided that I had left it in his apartment. What now? He took me to school and met me later only to tell me that his girlfriend destroyed all of my belongings. I was heart broken, but couldn't do anything about it. After I had gotten over this trauma, I started asking questions about the girl with the big pumps. Who was she, how did you meet her, and what does she do for a living? He explained that he met her in high school and she really showed him a lot of favor. She had money and could have any man she wanted.

She was talented, smart, and came from a "well-to-do" family, but she had a thing for young boys. "What do you mean she has a thing for young boys?" I asked. "Well, she was my high school English teacher." "You are kidding me," I said. "NO, I'm not, she's 35 and I'm 23. This car I'm driving she bought it. That's her apartment, and everything I own from my suits to my school books she buys." "Do you love her?" "No, but what's love got to do with it? I got what she needs and she got what I need." I didn't know what to think or feel at this point.

I don't know how Sandy was able to get back into the house, but all I know is that he never tried to take me back to that place. Somehow she got a hold to my mom's number and was calling there for me and harassing my mother. When I went to visit my mother she made it very clear to me that if I was going to date around, leave other people's men alone. She was sick of that woman calling there for me and cursing her out. Some time passed and Sandy was able to get me a job at the Hyatt. I started out as a room service order taker, and moved up to hosting in one of the Hyatt's finest restaurants. Although it was work, I was enjoying my job. I had a steady income, free food, and hope in getting my own place someday. Sandy and I were still friends, and I wanted to keep it that way.

One day he asked me if I wanted to get an apartment with him. He was tired of his current situation and was tired of being treated like a little boy by his "older woman." He told me that it was cool when he was in high school to have a teacher for his woman but now it was getting old. He said, "We don't have to date or anything, just share the bills. You can't afford to rent alone and neither can I. Now that you are

Recognize

working, we can put our money together." After thinking it
over a few days, and not having a lot of options, I thought it
was a good idea. We found a really nice place and things were
finally going well.

One evening Sandy asked me if I wanted to have sex.
"What kind of question is that? Do I want to have sex? Is
that all the game you got?" I asked him about the girl in his
music class, and the other girls that I'd seen him around
campus with, and he told me that he couldn't get any play
because we lived together. The honeys couldn't believe that we
were living together and not sleeping together. In short,
Sandy was trying to say that if it wasn't for me he could be
getting his groove on. I told him that he could get his groove
on anytime he wanted to. I didn't have anything to do with
his personal life, but he didn't see it that way. I started to see
his point after I met a really nice young man at the Hyatt
who was in town for business. He was one of IBM's young,
intelligent top executives who happened to be eating in my
restaurant every night. I couldn't help but notice him and he
also noticed me. One night he left me a key to his room and
asked me to meet him after I got off work. With Sandy
waiting for me outside, this deal didn't work out. Time went
on, things got weird and it was easier to date Sandy than to
date around one another.

It was time for me to get up for school. Sandy would
take me to school and drive me back and forth to work
everyday. This particular day, I was too sick to get up. I was
sick the next day, and the next day. I tried to pull myself
together because I didn't want to fall behind in school, so I
got up and went to school feeling like I was about to die. I
went to my Science class, and got some information on the

things I missed over the last three days. We were doing a blood analysis and for some strange reason, my test wasn't coming out as clear as everyone else's. I had my professor look at my results, and he told me that it's possible that I could be pregnant, and he highly recommended that I go get checked out. I left immediately, went to the free clinic and my pregnancy test came out positive. I was pregnant and in shock.

I went home and got in the bed because I was still very, very sick. The big vitamin pills they gave me to take, I couldn't get them down. As a matter of fact, I couldn't get anything down. The doctor told me that I had morning sickness. I told that doctor that I'm sick all day, not just in the morning. I was so sick that I couldn't eat, sleep, or think. All I could do was sit by the toilet and try to throw up my insides, because I didn't have anything in my stomach to throw up. In the first three months I lost twenty-five pounds, lost my job at the Hyatt for "no show" and fell way behind in school. The worst part of this pregnancy however was that Sandy would be missing in action for days. He would leave out in the morning and not return for three to four days at a time. I would be left in the house with no food and no way to get any. I couldn't think of anyone with a car, so all I did was pray and asked God that if I starved to death that He would make it painless. As I was praying a thought came to my mind. Call your friend from the Hyatt. He may still be in town, and maybe there's someway he could help you.

I later found out that Sandy's father had five kids by five different women and his mother had five kids by five different men. Sandy was well on his way in following in this family curse.

Recognize

He didn't see anything wrong with having babies all over Chicago; after all he had about nine step-brothers and sisters. The first thing I had to do was pray this curse off my son. Once I recognized that my son was labeled even before he came to this world, I knew that my work was cut out for me. Not to mention the ungodly soul tie that I developed with his dad. I wish I had someone around teaching me the real traps of the adversary; making it plain enough for me to understand. Demons were only famous actors and actresses in stage makeup getting paid big bucks to scare us at the box office, but the real deal is you don't have to go to the box office to see a demon, you could be living with a few.

A PRAYER FOR THE SINGLE AND PREGNANT

Lord forgive me for sinning against my own body. I know that my body is a temple and fornication is something You hate. Lord teach me how to walk in the Spirit and not after the flesh. I accept You as my Lord and Savior even in the state that I am in. I know that You are a life giver and I thank You for my unborn child. I know that sin comes with consequences, but Your love for me will cover a multitude of my sins. I know that You are a way-maker and I pray that in spite of my sin, that You would step in and restore. I know that You are able to make good what my sinful flesh and the devil have designed for bad. Because You are a life-giver, I take responsibility for my sins and for my unborn child and give my child back to You. Keep me, mold me and make me what You would have me to be as a person, a parent, and as a child of God. I may have turned my back on You many times, but thank You Lord for not turning Your back on me. As for me and my house, we will serve You Lord! In Jesus Name I Pray! AMEN!

Recognize

Meet the East Coast

I called the Hyatt and was connected to his room but he wasn't there so I left a message hoping that he would get it and return my call. Hours passed and I laid for the fourth day with no food to eat. The phone rang, I picked it up and when I heard his voice all I could do was cry. "What's the matter? Why haven't you been to work? Is everything OK? I was wondering if I would hear from you before I left. I will be going back home to New Jersey tomorrow, and I'm glad you called." I was so glad that he was doing all the talking because I was just to glad, sad, and emotional to say anything. All I could get out of my mouth is, "I need you to help me." My voice was very low and feeble. He became very quiet and compassionate. I could feel that he wanted to help me. He said, "What do you need for me to do? Just tell me and I will do it." I told him that I was pregnant, sick, hungry, and alone. He didn't question me, he just wanted to know what should he, could he, do. After a few more minutes of talking, he decided to take a cab to where I was. He brought me something to eat and $100. He also gave me his home phone number in New Jersey and told me to call him anytime I was in need. I felt like I had been touched by an angel.

I had five more months of pregnancy to go. Sandy's behavior was the same at home two days turned into four to five days. I couldn't work and had to drop out of school, so my life consisted of TV and walks to the lake front. My New Jersey friend sent money every month to make sure that I had food to eat and money for any emergencies. Sandy didn't really care about my condition. He felt that since he now had to pay the entire rent and utilities, he was doing more than

Recognize

his fair share. After all, he was just with a woman who did everything for him.

It was a bright summer day and Sandy was in a good mood. "Why don't you get dressed and I'll take you out for a little lunch." The baby was due anyday, and I really wanted to get out of the house. I felt like I had been in there doing a life sentence. We were near downtown at a fast food burger place and my stomach was feeling a little crappy. As I sat there, I began to feel worse. A little old white lady asked, "Are you in labor?" "I don't know, the baby isn't due for another week." The little old lady told Sandy to get me to a hospital. Sandy said, "I can drop you off, but I can't stay. I got to get to work." He dropped me off at the hospital. They kept me and started preparing me for delivery. Sandy visited twice while I was in labor. My labor was so long I thought I was going to die; even the doctors were getting a little concerned.

The labor and delivery was really, really hard. The pains were strong, but I wasn't dilating. I remember telling one of the nurses that I saw a program that showed if you focus and breath, that it would help the pain, but this technique wasn't working for me, and if she could give me something for the pain I would really appreciate it. She said she would check with my doctor, and never came back. About forty minutes later, they wanted me to push, but every time I would push they would lose the baby's heartbeat on the monitor. My pushing would put the baby into distress. Everyone in the room had a very worried look on their faces and no one would tell me what was going on. Every now and then a little Chinese woman would walk over to me, rub my face and ask "Is there anyone coming to see about you?" "Yes, the baby's daddy will be here when he gets off work," I kept saying. The look on her face was telling me that neither I or the baby weren't going to make it. I really wasn't scared; I almost didn't want to make it. I really wanted to die and just get this life over with.

It's time to push again. Every time I would push all the bells and whistles would go off, and people would start running around screaming code blue, code red, and all I could remember is much pain and agony. The doctor said that if they didn't get that baby out soon, he needed to take other measures. All the while, everyone was speaking in codes. They brought in a silver table with all kinds of instruments and everyone were getting into position. Next thing I know, I felt a pain so great that I screamed "WHAT ARE YOU DOING? WHAT ARE YOU DOING?" The Chinese nurse was holding my hand and speaking in her language. I think she was praying for me in Chinese. I felt like a little lamb being taken to the slaughter. I looked in the mirror that they positioned down below and could see that the doctor had cut a hole in me large enough for five kids to slide out. Everyone in the labor room shouted "PUSH, PUSH, PUSH". I was in so much pain, tired, closer to death than life, that I said in a very feeble voice, "I'd rather die, I am not pushing anymore!"

Obviously, this was not an option. The doctor said to his staff, "She's giving up, let's just take the baby." They handed him something that looked like two large salad spoons, and he inserted them and tried to pull the baby out, but something was holding the baby back. He removed the spoons, and inserted his hand and discovered that the cord was wrapped around the baby's neck. He removed the cord,

Recognize

reinserted the spoons and pulled the baby out. All the while I'm screaming, "NO! NO! NO! STOP! STOP! You're Hurting Me! You're Hurting Me! You're Hurting Me!" The entire staff was trying to pin me down and keep me in position, all I wanted to do was get up and leave, and leave all that pain, blood and agony behind. I wanted out! After what appeared to be two additional hours more worth of trauma and chaos, the doctor managed to pull the baby out. They rushed the baby off and were still doctoring on me for about another hour.

The next day, the doctor came to see about me and I didn't want to talk to him. I didn't want to talk to anyone. The doctor stood at my bedside and spoke to me anyway, but very softly. He apologized for what he had to put me through. He said, "Toni, I know we hurt you. The cord was wrapped around the baby's neck and we didn't realize it until you were already in labor for forty hours. I know that you didn't want a C-section, but if I had known that the cord was wrapped around the baby's neck, we would have given you one. The baby is doing fine, he just has a knot on his head from the forceps we used to pull him out. I need you to eat something, and try to get up and walk around." He seemed like he was at my bedside for about thirty minutes just talking to the air, because I wasn't responding to him at all. They were concerned that I was slipping into a condition called "post partum blues," a type of depression that new mothers experience. In my opinion, I just felt like the hospital staff was trying to kill me. I wouldn't speak to anyone who entered my room. When anyone would come into my room I would turn my head to the other side and just stare at the walls, and wouldn't say anything to them or even acknowledge that anyone was even in the room.

One day a nurse came into my room and brought the baby. She told me to feed him and talk to him. She said that it was important that we bond before I could leave the hospital. I acted like no one was in the room and that she couldn't be talking to me. I could hear her walking away, but wasn't sure if she left the baby until I heard his little voice. I turned just to see what he looked like, and paged the nurse station for someone to get him. The nurse came into my room to see why I paged her, but when she would ask what she could do, I wouldn't say a word. I would just look at her and roll my eyes and pout. What I really wanted to say was, "Y'ALL HURT ME, Y'ALL TRIED TO KILL ME, Y'ALL DIDN'T TELL ME THAT IT WOULD BE THIS BAD. I HATE ALL Y'ALL. LEAVE ME ALONE, YOU TAKE THIS BABY, AND YOU FEED HIM, ISN'T THAT WHAT Y'ALL ARE BEING PAID FOR, AND WHILE YOU'RE AT IT, DON'T COME IN HERE ANY MORE!" But instead, I just didn't say a word. I wouldn't eat, talk, or walk. I guess I had the blues.

They called my mother to tell her about my condition. They told her that if I didn't get better, that she would have to take the baby or some other responsible adult for a little while. The nurse explained that they couldn't send a baby home with a young mother with "Post Partum Blues." My mother sat and talked to me for a while. She made it clear that she wasn't going to take no newborn baby home with her, and that I needed to get myself together. I didn't look her way, or say anything. Everyone was standing around to see if I would speak. I was speaking on the inside. I had a lot to say on the inside, I just didn't have anything to say to the people on the outside. I really just wanted everyone to disappear and leave me alone.

Recognize

Later on that evening they brought the baby into my room. This time I looked at the baby and even picked him up. I wanted to see what his knot looked like. I removed his little cap and saw where the forceps had hurt his little head. He looked at me and smiled. I was surprised that I liked him. He was cute, soft, and friendly, but after a while he started to cry and I didn't know what to do, so I put him back down into his plastic little bed and paged the nurse to come get him. The nurse's station saw that it was me again and they ignored my page. They wanted me and the baby to bond. This was my sixth day in the hospital and they were not satisfied with my behavior. After about a half hour of no reply from the nurse's station, I laid on the pager button to make sure that I was getting someone's attention. After about one hour, a black nurse came in and asked me if I needed her to take the baby. I said, "WHAT YOU THINK?" and turned my head toward the wall. She took the baby and left.

Twenty minutes had passed and my regular nurse came in and said, "You have been giving us all a fit. We know you wanted us to get the baby, but we wanted you to spend some time with him for a while. Your time is up and I'm here to get him." "Where is he?" she asked. I said, "Another nurse came and got him already." "What nurse? There are only three of us on duty and we were all instructed to leave you with the baby for a while. In addition we would have taken the entire bed, not just the baby." She stormed out of my room and the entire nursery ward was up in arms. I stepped into the hallway to see what the matter was. I saw police, nurses, and other staff members just looking at me as if they or I were crazy. I just got back into bed. My nurse walked into my room with a police officer, and they wanted me to describe the lady who took my baby. After much questioning and chaos, a cop walked into my room and said, "We got her." I found out later that there was a woman on my floor who lost her baby in delivery about two days ago, and she wanted a baby so bad that she was trying to take mine home with her.

They kept me in the hospital for another week, but they sent my son home with my mother. I know that they thought I was going crazy, or already crazy, but I thought that they were just as crazy. I didn't trust any of them. They were just a group of killers in white and green outfits trying to kill me alive. The only good thing about being there was that I had a bed to sleep in every night, and three meals that I could count on even if I didn't eat half the stuff they brought me.

When I got home, I called my mother to check on the baby. She would say he's doing fine. One day I called her to check on the baby, and she asked me if I wanted to see him. I hadn't thought about that. I didn't know what I would do if I saw him. I didn't know if the baby would like me, or if he would wonder who I was. The baby was only a month old, but I didn't know much about babies, so I didn't know if seeing him was a good idea, but I said yes anyway. When I walked into my mother's apartment, my sisters were all looking at me to see if the crazy lady would appear, or to see how me and the baby would interact. I said, "Where is the baby?" My mother said, "Your son is in the back bedroom." I thought wow, I have a son, which sounded weird to me. As I walked to the back bedroom my sisters trailed me to get an up close and personal view of what would happen next. The baby was just laying there cooing and looking. I sat on the bed next to him and wanted to touch him, but didn't know if

Recognize

it was okay. My sister said, " You can touch him, he won't bite." I smiled because I was just thinking about touching him and it was just like she was reading my mind. I touched his foot and it was a real foot. I touched his hand and it was like a real hand, but just soft. He almost looked like a toy doll, just real. I got into his face to see who he looked like and to my surprise, he looked just like me. I was thinking to myself, I may like this baby. All of a sudden, the baby smiled. It was the biggest and the prettiest smile I had ever seen. I looked at my sister and said, "I think this baby likes me. You think he likes me?" I asked. My sister said, "YES, I think he likes you!" My mother wanted a report on how I was doing around the baby, and they told her that I was just looking into his face. She walked back in the room, picked the baby up and put him into my arms. I wasn't ready for that, but it turned out okay. It was almost like he enjoyed being in my arms better than just laying down on the bed.

It was time to feed him, so I tried to pass him off to my sister, and my mother suggested that I feed him. I was afraid that I wouldn't do it right and my mother would scream at me and call me stupid or something; but to my surprise, she told me that she was sure that I would do it right and handed me a warm bottle to put into the baby's mouth. This wasn't so bad. The baby sucked on the bottle until all the milk was gone and then he fell asleep. I really liked visiting with him. I went back to my apartment up North, and just thought about the face of that little boy. I called my mother more and more to check on the baby, and to see if I could visit again. She told me that I could visit any time. I would love it when the baby would smile at me. I felt like he knew I was his mother.

One day I was at home watching the news and there had been a drive-by shooting right in front of my mother's house. Five little girls had been shot while they were outside jumping rope. They showed my mother's building and then switched to a scene at the hospital. It was my mother. She was on TV. One of the five girls was my little sister. I was in shock. I didn't have a way to the hospital, so I kept calling around to find out more details and to see where the baby was. There were so many traumas in my life, and my mother was such a nervous wreck, that when I finally made it over to her apartment, she told me to take the baby home with me. I didn't know if that was a good idea, because I didn't know anything about a baby. How do I know when to feed it, or how would I know how to change it? How do I clean it, etc? My mother told me to just call her if I had any questions. My neighbor upstairs helped out a lot and after about one month, things got easier. I started to like being a mommy. My little sister was alright. All five girls were shot with be-be guns and all were sent home the same night except for one of the girls who got shot in the eye. They put her eye out. If it had been real bullets, it would have been worse for all five victims.

My son was three months now, and I was tired of sitting in the house and wondering where our next meal was going to come from. I think that my friend from New Jersey was getting tired of hearing all of my drama stories also. He really didn't mind the money part because he had so much of it. One day he asked me what did I want to do with my life. I told him that I either wanted to be a nurse, a dancer, or a businesswoman. He said, "Why don't you be a dancing nurse?" and we both laughed about it. Then he suggested since Chicago wasn't dealing me such a great hand, why don't

Recognize

I move to Jersey, me and the baby, and start over. I had never been out of town, or on a plane, and didn't know if that was such a good idea. He told me to think about it and get back with him.

He told me that he had his own place, but the only thing was that his parents were real religious. We would have to tell them that the baby was his, and that we would be getting married soon. I didn't know if that was such a great idea, but these were his parents and I wasn't going to get in the middle. I was grateful that he was making such a big investment in me. There wasn't anything in Chicago for me, so I decided to go. I told a few of my friends, my mother, and my sisters that I was moving out of town. Mr. New Jersey had a cab pick me and the baby up at my apartment, along with as much as I could pack, and off to the airport we went. This was my first time on a plane and I really enjoyed it. When I arrived at my friend's parent's house, they made a really big fuss over the baby. My friend only had one sister who was a physical therapist, a beautiful mother who was a great cook and a hard working father. Their house was very large and everyone was so friendly.

When I made it to his place, I noticed that he only had one bedroom. It was a very nice one bedroom condo. I asked him where were the baby and I were going to sleep. He told me that we could have his bedroom and he would take the couch. This man was so nice to me that I couldn't dare take his bedroom, so I told him that I would take the couch, and get the baby a baby's bed. I didn't want him on the couch after all he was doing for me, and plus he was a big time IBM employee; he needed to be well rested. I also didn't want to cramp his style as I had done so many people in the past.

Things were trying to look up. His parents didn't want me to get a job right away. They felt that I should spend a little more time with the baby. Their family was really supportive of one another, close and everyone did what mom and dad told them to do. This was a little new for me. I was used to running my own messed up life. One day I overheard my friend on the phone. It sounded like he was in an argument with someone. About one hour later, there was knocking and banging at the door. He told me not to answer it. It finally stopped. I looked through the peephole and didn't see anyone, so I opened the door. Then I found pictures in picture frames of my friend and some woman. This must be his girlfriend I thought, and he is having a hard time explaining who I am and why I'm living with him. I felt bad for him.

I walked into his bedroom and brought him all the broken pictures and ripped letters and cards and just laid them on his bed and walked out. He called me "Toni, come here." I walked back in and sat on the bed and just waited for him to talk. He said, "This is someone I used to date. I told her all about you. She knows your situation and is being unreasonable. She's a little psycho anyway, so I don't want you to worry about any of this. I have everything under control." I wanted to speak, but I didn't know what to say. I understood where the woman in the picture was coming from, but on the other hand, I needed a place for me and my son to stay. I asked, "Do you love her?" I asked because I wanted to know if I was causing any pain in his life. To my surprise, he said, "I thought I did, until I met you." I didn't know what to say behind that statement. I liked him. I really appreciated what he was doing for me, and if my life wasn't full of so much trauma and drama, I could have maybe

Recognize

possibly loved him too. However, I just needed more "me" time, more mommy-son time, and more time getting to know who I was and where I was going before trying to operate in love. I felt a little confused. I felt like I owed him a lot, but I really wasn't ready to give any of me, so I put my efforts into cleaning and staying out of his way. Basically, I tried to avoid the love scene.

One afternoon, he called me and told me that we had a dinner party to go to. This was something that he and his big shot co-workers did once a month. He wanted me to put on something nice, and be ready by 5:30pm. He had already arranged for his mother to keep the baby, which she really enjoyed doing. When he got there, he asked me why I wasn't dressed, but I was dressed. The best thing I had was a pair of black pants and a white shirt. This was part of my Hyatt Hotel uniform. It was clean, pressed, and I thought I was looking okay. He said, "It's too late to take you shopping, so let's go. You should have told me that you didn't have any clothes." I could tell that he was a little pissed off, so I didn't say much. I didn't want to make things worse. We arrived at a big beautiful house. The woman who answered the door was plain but pretty, friendly, and had great taste in furniture. I just stood at the front door until she said, "Take a seat. You can sit anywhere you like." I felt a little out of place. Everyone was college graduate. They all had some type of impressive career, and were married and living large. I had a glass of wine which I held on to all night, and I wasn't looking to tell anything about myself. Everyone had such success stories. I prayed to God that no one would ask me anything about who I was, and what I did, or what college I graduated from. Their lives were so pure, happy, and prosperous. I didn't want to bring the spirit of the dinner party down. All the women had on huge wedding rocks, and they seemed to be very happy.

"Toni, you're so quiet. What is it like in Chicago?" one woman asked. I was thinking, this is an easy question. As long as I don't have to talk about myself, I can get through this night. I chimed in with the girls and tried to fit in as best I could. It was time to eat. The table was spread for a king and his guests. It felt like Thanksgiving there was so much food. I couldn't believe that this career woman with two children came home from a hard day's work and cooked all this food. I thought to myself she must be super woman. I totally felt out of my league. After a while I became more relaxed and actually had fun.

Every month we visited a different house, ate, talked, and enjoyed good conversation. One evening I received a phone call from the man of the house, and he asked me what was for dinner. I started laughing because I hadn't cooked since I'd been in Jersey, in addition, the best I could do was a great hamburger or some awesome tuna fish salad. But, he wasn't playing. He told me that it was our turn to entertain the young executive club and I needed to have something ready by 6:00pm for five couples. I panicked and knew immediately that I wouldn't be able to pull off the type of meals the other ladies had done. Everything in our freezer was frozen and I didn't have any money to go grocery shopping. I really wasn't expecting this tonight. I felt like this night was going to be an embarrassment to my friend and me. I prayed to God, "What should I do?" I decided to order a whole bunch of Chinese food. I could call it a casual day. We had a small place, plus everyone couldn't sit at the table so we would do something a little different. My creativity went into overdrive.

Recognize

When he got home, he said, "I don't smell anything cooking." I told him to relax and just trust me. Our guests started to arrive, and from the looks on their faces they too were wondering where's the food. I made an announcement that we decided to do something a little different. Right at that moment about three Chinese men walked in with boxes of assorted Chinese food and cookies. My guests loved this idea. I looked at my friend and he smiled. He was pleased that our guests all loved Chinese food. One of the young ladies said, "This is a great idea, I've always wanted to do something like this, but didn't know how it would go over. The dinners I went to after my husband and I had ours they were all sit down dinners, and to be honest, I was beginning to hate these monthly gatherings. It was taking a lot out of me." "Me too, me too, me too," everyone started to say. I felt like a hero. I looked up to heaven and whispered, "Thank You God." We ate, played games, and talked stuff all night.

I felt like I was in a fairytale relationship without all the hassle until one night it happened. I was asked a series of questions that were leading up to "the sex talk." I really found him handsome, funny, friendly and a overall great catch. He even reminded me how many very successful women who would love to be in my shoes, meaning being his mate, and I was acting like I didn't know what I had. I really did know that I was lucky to have someone taking care of me, but I needed a little more time, but my time was running out. Could I lay there and just do it, just to live in peace, or do I take a stand and just say NO, or do I keep avoiding the issue and hope that it will just go away? My immature mind said, "Just wait it out, and it'll go away."

One day he came home; and he looked like he'd had a rough day. I had just put my son to sleep and asked if I could get him anything. "Yes, some love," he replied. I wasn't ready for that answer, so I just went into the kitchen and brought him something to drink. I was wondering what was wrong with me. "I didn't ask for anything to drink," he said. "I think you know what I want. You're not a little girl; you're an adult now, so act like one." I agreed that I wasn't a little girl. I could sense that this was the beginning of a huge argument. After exchanging many words, he told me to take a shower because tonight he was going to get him some. I acted like I didn't hear him and just laid across the bed hoping that he would just fall asleep. It wasn't that I didn't find him attractive or appealing. It was just too soon for me. All I could remember was the pain I endured from childbirth, and the thought of going through that again just turned me off. I just wasn't ready for the responsibilities of sex. He tried to force himself on me and I asked him to stop. I really wanted him to understand my emotional state and he really wanted me to understand his needs. Our wires were crossed and the only way he could express himself was through anger. He hit me in the face with his fist and then again in the chest. After a while I stopped counting the number of blows I encountered. All I remember is that I was blocking my face and trying to endure this beating. I was more willing to take the beating than to have sex against my will. Next he ran out the house, got in his car and left. I was so shocked that I laid in the bed for about one hour before I could move. My face was bloody, my eye was turning black, and my entire body was in pain. As I looked in the mirror at myself, I couldn't recognize the person in it. I looked a mess, I felt sad, I felt like this ride is now over, and it's time to get off. Where would I go? Who can I call? How can I get some money?

185

Recognize

The spirit of rejection that was on him turned him into a woman beater.

This man felt rejected by me. I wasn't trying to operate in nothing but survival, and was still trying to figure out how to take care of me and a baby. I was caught in a catch 22; living with another man who wanted me to play wife or living out in the street with a baby. I knew God, but I didn't know His phone number. I didn't know that all I had to do was call on His name and He would hear my cry. I was carnal, and needed to be spiritual.

I picked up the phone and called his mother and explained to her what had just happened. She already knew. Her son was at her house in a panic. He thought I was dead. After what felt like the twentieth blow, I stop screaming. "Are you alright?" she asked, "NO!" I said. I felt like every bone in my face and chest was broken and I didn't want to stay there. She came and got me to have a family meeting. "A FAMILY MEETING, WHAT THE HELL FOR?" I was wondering. She explained to me that that's how they handled things in their family, by discussing it. He spoke first. "Well, what happened Ma, I had been asking Toni for sex for a while, and she's been walking around doing nothing while I work everyday. I brought her here from Chicago, and I'm taking care of her and her son." His mother said, "What do you mean her and her son? I thought Ajani was your son too." Now the truth came out. After about two hours of discussion, the mother decided that it would be better for me to stay in their four bedroom house until we could all figure out what to do next. This would give her son time to figure out what he wanted to do with his life in terms of companionship and it would give me time to get over my many, many wounds. It would also give her more time around the baby, and keep some of the drama down. Even through all of my emotional scars, I was tripping on the fact that he was having a sex conversation with his parents. I didn't think people at least black people, had open discussion about sex with their parents.

I called home to tell my mother what I was going through and that I wanted to come home, but she felt that I was in the best place for now. I was with a family who loved me and the baby. I was in a big house with a family who not only had the money to take care of us, but who wanted to. She felt that I was in the right place, but for some odd reason, I felt like I was in hell. I had no friends, no car to get around, no money to buy ice cream and no one to talk to. I had the urge to go to church, but I had no way to get there, no idea where one was, and I really didn't want anyone seeing me until my face got back to normal. With nothing left to do, I just cried myself to sleep one more night.

I spent most of my time upstairs in the guest bedroom. Every now and then I would look over the upstairs bannister to watch the family play with my baby. They all seemed to be having a great time. I stayed out of the way as to not make any mistakes that would put me back into the street. They called me down for breakfast and dinner. One morning at breakfast, the sister asked me if I was going to spend the rest of my life in that bedroom. I told her that I would like to get a job, and if she could bring a newspaper home from work I would appreciate it. One thing led to another and I ended up working at a hotel in New York. I worked for a year. This was enough time for me to save a little cash to make my way back to Chicago. But before I leave this chapter of my life, I must tell you about the witches I met in New York. Yes real witches, the ones who sit up and do spells and burn candles to make evil things happen.

Recognize

Meet the Witch

I finally got me a job. It wasn't much but it allowed me to buy a few personal items and save money so that I could one day move back to Chicago. I was a cashier at a hotel restaurant. The waitresses would bring me their checkout slips along with the money from their tables for me to check them out and give them their change and tips for the evening. One of the waitresses was shaking like she had just seen a ghost and she handed me her slip. I just figured she was having a bad day. Some of the other girls were saying that she was in some type of trouble. "What type of trouble?" I asked. "Well, she pissed Franky off," one of the girls said. Franky is in witch-school and she is going to burn some black candles on her tonight, and Cindy is very worried about it." I thought that that was the most ridiculous thing I had ever heard. So, when Franky walked up to me to check out, I asked her if it was true that she was a witch. "Who wants to know?" she asked. "I do," I said. "Yes, I've been studying for three years and I know how to do spells, burn candles and make a few other things happen if I want to." "Like what?" I asked. "Like whatever I want." "Why are you asking anyway? Aren't you a church girl?" "How do you know what I am?" I asked. She said, "We learn how to spot y'all 'God worshipers.'" I know that you are having a problem with an ex-boyfriend, and if you want me to, I can burn a candle tonight and tell you what the problem is." "I thought that your candles were just for bad things, and to put spells on people." "My candles can be used to break spells too, or for whatever I want them to be used for. So what do you say?" "Hey, go for it, what do I have to lose?" I really didn't think that I was having ex-boyfriend problems, or that I needed to

Recognize

have a spell broken off me. It was going to be very interesting to see what she was going to come up with.

This witch was a friendly person for the most part. White, with black roots and a bad blonde hair color job. Her teeth needed to be whiten, and she always wore black. She wasn't an ugly girl, but she wasn't pretty either. I think that by my knowing that she was a witch made me look at her a little different. "Hey, "T", you ready for what I found out?" "Yes," I said. "Well, you used to date some man named Sandy, and he used to date an older woman who practiced witchcraft, and when he was with her he learned some stuff himself. I know you used to live with him, and while you all were living together he did something to you that caused you to always call other men by his name, and even though you never loved him, you think about him all the time. The only way you can break this spell is by going back to Chicago, and take back what he took from you and destroying it." I was in shock. I thought that she was going to tell me something about my New Jersey friend, not reach back all the way in Chicago and tell me something about Sandy. Her feedback sounded just like prophecy; the type of prophecy that I was accustomed to hearing in the church. I was glad to have this information, but I noticed right away that witches were very similar to the prophets in the church. I made arrangements to go to Chicago and meet with Sandy to get a hold of the object in question. I destroyed it and I felt good about the discovery. On the other hand however, I became very concerned about the witchcraft because it were very, very similar to prophecy, so I began to ask God to help me discern between the two spirits. Franky made it clear to me that she would not be burning anymore candles with my name on it because it was a major task for her when dealing with God's people. Her conversations were interesting, but I wanted to make sure that I stayed on the LORD's side, so I didn't entertain a relationship with her.

Witches get their help from Satan, while saints get theirs from the Lord. If you choose to get help from Satan, you will also inherent everything else he has to offer, like harassment, sickness, disease, and lots of disappointment. He has some power (but not over the believer), and will give it and take it away, but our Father who's in heaven has all power. If you've ever practiced witchcraft, or participated in the occult, you must loose yourself from him, ask for forgiveness from God, and choose the things of God, and not the lies of Satan.

Recognize

A PRAYER FOR SPIRITUAL DISCERNMENT

Father God, in the mighty Name of Jesus, I pray that I will be able to tell the difference between a witch and a prophet. Your Word tells us to try the spirit by the Spirit of God, and that everyone who says Lord, Lord isn't of You, Father. Lord, I pray that You would sharpen my spiritual eyes, and help me to see and discern these spirits that are not of You. I pray that as I walk in the authority of Jesus Christ of Nazareth that I would bring down Satan's kingdom and walk in faith with Holy Ghost Wisdom and Power. Teach me how to wear and apply every piece of the spiritual armor and cover my back in cases where Satan has me surrounded. Give me Your strength, Your grace, and Your anointing to tear down the adversary's camp. I pray that You cover me with Your blood from the crown of my head to the soles of my feet. In Jesus' Name I pray! AMEN!

My First Apartment

I finally got myself together, and was able to land a job up north in Chicago at a bank as a teller. My first apartment was a studio apartment with only my clothes, a mattress, and paper plates and cups. I enjoyed having my own apartment, but I missed my baby. They thought that it would be a good idea for me to leave him in New Jersey until I got myself together. Three things stick out in my mind about my first apartment. The day that I moved in I had to make my way past two large women outside fighting, cursing at each other, and pulling out each other's hair. I was just trying to mind my business and get into the elevator to get to my studio apartment. After getting my last box out the car, one of the women who was in the fight was on the elevator checking out her scars, and asking me what the f--k I was looking at. I told her that I was not trying to do anything but move into my apartment. I was letting her know I wasn't in the mood for any B.S., but I also wasn't in the mood to fight someone twice my size. We both got off on the same floor. She went her way, and I went mine. After getting settled in, I noticed that I could see into my neighbor's window. It was the girl on the elevator. She had company every night with a different man. I saw a little girl too. I didn't know she had a little girl. It had been a long day, and it was time for me to go to sleep. My apartment was quiet for the most part; the only entertainment I had was my radio and the activity that was going on in the window across the way. I was saving up for a TV.

The next day I left out early to make it to work on time. My neighbor was already up and out. She was sitting outside

Recognize

just looking. "Good morning" I said. She said "Hi" and turned her head. I went to work for eight hours and when I returned she was sitting in the same spot. "Good evening," I said. She said "Hi". This went on everyday for about two weeks. Then one evening, she asked me, "Why are you so friendly? People are not friendly around here, and every time you see me you say, hello, or good morning, or some sh-- like that. Where are you from anyway?" "I'm from the Westside of Chicago. I'm just trying to be nice. What's up with you?" I asked. When I first met you, you were out here beating up some chick, and then after that, every time I see you, you're with a different man, or either just sitting out here chilling. What do you do for a living?" "None of your damn business," she said. "I do what I have to do to keep food on my table and to keep a place over my daughter's head." After putting two and two together, I knew she was a hooker.

One day I was on my way to the grocery store and Linda, (yes her name was Linda) was sitting outside just chilling as usual. "Hey, I'm about to go to the grocery store. Do you want to come?" "Yeah, I need a few things." When we returned, she had a few customers outside our complex waiting for her. They tried to offer me some business, but that was not my field. "No thanks!" I said. "I would pay you double," one of the men said. "No thanks, I'll pas. Linda was busy for the rest of the night. Linda was such a smart girl and seemed like she could make something more of herself. I began to ask her lots of questions, like what made her go this route? Where was her little girl when she was working, how much did she get paid? I wanted to know did she ever get beat up, would she ever consider doing something else for a living? In short, she wasn't interested. She said that her mother told her that she would never be anything, and thought her

194

brothers were everything. "What if I told you that your mother is a liar, and that you could turn out to be somebody?" She said, "If you call my mother out of her name again, I'm going to kick your a--." She was too violent for me. I didn't want to have to cut her, so I kept my distance for a while. People say that the Westside is bad, but the Northside of Chicago has every type of crime on the planet operating. There were so many territorial demons on the Northside that you would not believe.

One day a friend of mine came by to see if I wanted a used typewriter that his company was giving away. "Sure," I said. I used that typewriter often to update my resume and to practice my typing so that one day I could get a better job. I went from being a teller at the bank to a personal banker. Things were looking a little better even though I still only had a mattress and a radio. I hadn't gotten a TV yet. At the bank we could win little prizes for positive customer comment card, and other job performance areas. The Vice President of the bank won a 13 inch black and white TV. The employees of the bank were all wondering how he won the TV. It got to a point that the employees didn't go out of there way for good customer service because only top management was winning all of the good prizes. I was at my desk when he won the prize, and he came over to me and said, "I heard that you were trying to win the 13 inch TV. Yeah, but I'm sure with an important job like yours, you deserved it more so than me." The VP was a short fat man. He looked like a black Pillsbury Doe Boy, and he had to be 20 years my senior. He said to me, "I really don't need another TV. My wife and I have about five color TVs so you can have it. I will take it to your car when you get off work." and then he walked away. I asked myself, did he just offer me

Recognize

a free TV? Wow, this is my lucky day. I was so excited. I was thinking that I needed to go out and buy a stand for my new TV. Work was over and he was already at my car with the box in his hand. He asked me if I would need any help with getting the TV to my apartment. "NO," I said, "and thanks, I really needed a TV."

When I got home, I ripped open the box and plugged in my new TV. I was wondering if Linda could see the light coming from my apartment. I wanted her to see my new TV. Neither of us had curtains. I could see all of her business and she could see mine. I watched TV all night. I was almost late for work trying to watch the morning news. When I arrived at the bank, the VP asked me how was I enjoying the TV. I told him that I was enjoying the TV just fine. He asked me if he could come over sometime and watch it with me. I found that question a little strange especially with a man with five color TV's at home. I told him that I was hardly at home. He said, "Well when you are at home, maybe I can come over." I started feeling sick to my stomach. I knew there was a catch to the free TV. My grandmother would always tell me there's nothing in life that's free. Then I could here Joann telling me that one day I would use my body for a free meal or for something else. The devil is a liar, I was thinking. The only way I would let this man in my house is for him to come and pick up his TV. For days and weeks he hounded me about coming to my apartment to watch a 13 inch black and white TV. I told him that I didn't have any furniture, and that my apartment wasn't set up for company, but he still wanted to come by. He asked me one day, "Is this how you treat people that are nice to you? I think you better reconsider your decision. I can make things a little difficult for you around here." I was mad and felt stupid for falling for the old "let me give you a TV trick." The bad thing about it was he didn't even buy the TV. He won it and probably cheated to get it. I never heard of a company giving out employee incentives to a VP; their salaries were enough.

He walked past my desk and whispered "I'm waiting." I went to his desk after thinking long and hard about it and asked him, "What is it that you want from me? Do you want me to pay you for the TV or what?" He said, "I just want to come by and watch a little TV with you, that's all." "That's all!" I asked. "Yes! That's all." Of course I didn't feel comfortable about this, but I gave him my address and apartment number and told him that he could come over and watch a little TV with me tonight. He got there about 7pm with some expensive wine. I told him that I didn't drink wine and besides, I didn't have any glasses. "No problem, I just don't believe in coming to someone's house empty-handed. I was in shorts and a T-shirt. I had already gotten out of my work clothes. He was still in his bank suit that was too little, and he tried to sit on my mattress which was almost the same as sitting on the floor. He looked stupid sitting there, I felt crazy, and we both just sat there waiting to see what would happen next. So after about two hours, I turned to him and said, "Well I hope you enjoyed watching TV with me. I guess I will see you tomorrow at work." I stood up as a signal that it was time for him to leave and then I watched him struggle off the floor/mattress. I walked him to the door, by simply taking one big giant step, opened the door and was waiting for him to walk out. He just stood at the door looking at me. I said "Oh, don't forget your wine." The next thing I knew he is trying to kiss me in the mouth. I asked him, "What are you doing?" He said, "Don't act like you're innocent." I pushed, he pulled. I prayed that this man would not try to

Recognize

rape me. I thought I was home free after getting him to the door. He said, "Give me back my TV." He snatched it out the wall and stormed out with it in his hands. Now I was back to a quiet, dark apartment, but dealing with him everyday was not worth keeping the TV.

The treatment at work was not good and I knew I was going to have to find another job. What the devil meant for evil, God made it for my good. I ended up getting a better job with a phone company that started my telecommunications career. The devil was always trying to get me to be a product of my environment, but money, sex and things etc; couldn't separate me from the Love of God. The devil was trying to tell me to go ahead, sleep with him, no one will know. There are a lot of things that women can do for money, but I told the devil that he could keep the TV and every other ungodly offer coming my way. I believed with prayer I could get a better job and I did. I've seen people all my life sell their bodies and make compromises for the things of this world, but I believed that God would supply all of my needs according to His riches in glory by Christ Jesus, and I didn't have to sell nothing to get it. I don't have to date men for money, I don't have to steal and I don't have to lie. All I have to do is stand on the promises of God. After a short while, I bought me a color TV and a few more things for my place.

Men can be whores too! Women sell their bodies for sex and men give money and material things for sex. The Bible say's that the love of money is the root of all evil. The love of ungodly sex is a result of evil thoughts and actions, Gody sex is a gift from God and it is only for people married to each other. Anytime we relay on things, money, sex and other fleshly pleasures to make us who we are, or to get what we want, we are telling our God that we don't need Him that we don't need to use faith, we can buy what we want or manipulate others to get what we want. This is ungodly and has Satan's name written all over it. You better recognize!

There was a knock at my door. When I opened the door it was Linda. One of her customers had beat her and raped her, and took all of her money. She looked a mess. I helped her clean herself up and had a long talk with her. I was trying to get her to find something else to do for money, like get a job. She cried and cried and told me that she didn't have any skills. I told her if she was serious about changing careers that I would help her after work by teaching her how to type and how to pass an interview. I would also help her with her attire. All of her outfits were hooker gear low cut tops with mini skirts. Night after night, Linda spent time at my apartment pecking at the typewriter, and showing me her progress. After several months of coaching I told Linda that I knew some people at a bank that I used to work at that may give her an interview. We went shopping for a suit and did something suitable with her hair and worked a little on her walk. She had long legs and walked like she was in a glamour girl fashion show. She needed to tone it down a little, less booty action, and more sophistication. We worked on her resume and added a few extras and prayed that God would do it for her. She stopped by my apartment that morning for me to give her a look-over, and I told her to, "Go get them." She was a little fearful and doubtful, and all she could remember were the words from her mother telling her that she would never be anything. She asked me, "Do you really think I could get a real job?" I said, "I don't think, I know." "Well, do you think your God will come through for me too?" "My God is your God if you want him to be," I said. "Yes, I want

Recognize

Him to be." We prayed, and we both went on our ways.

When I got home, I could see this nice looking woman sitting in Linda's spot all dressed up in a nice blue suit. I almost didn't recognize Linda. "So, what happened?" I asked. She looked down to the ground with a very sad look and told me that all that hard work was a waste of time, I felt horrible. "Maybe next time," I said. She jumped up and said, "GOT CHA! I'm just kidding, I GOT THE JOB! I GOT THE JOB!" We both jumped up and down and screamed until we both lost our voices. It was a Friday evening and a wonderful way to start the weekend. That Saturday morning Linda came over with some hot biscuits and some other breakfast food. "Girl, did you cook all this stuff?" I asked. "Yes, I'm a great cook. I just didn't have a whole lot of time to do it in the past." "Well, thanks this is going to hit the spot." I said. I was just thinking what I was going to do for breakfast. Then, she handed me a card from her purse. It was a thank you card. "No problem, it was my pleasure to help you." I said. Then she tried to kiss me in the mouth. "Woe, woe, what's up with the kiss? I don't flow like that." She looked surprised over my reaction. From her world, she thought that that was a normal way to show her appreciation. I told her that the biscuits and the card was enough. She didn't understand my behavior, and I truly didn't understand hers. She said, "I never known anyone like you. Someone that was willing to help me get off the streets and find a nice job. Most women I know are in competition. I feel like I love you." I had to explain to her that there are different kinds of love. You have Agape, which is unconditional love, Eros which is a romantic love, and Philia which is a brotherly love. And there are more ways than using your body to show that you love a person. I introduced Linda to church and she was well on her way to a new beginning.

Now when I left out to go to work there was no more Linda. She was out early taking her daughter to the baby sitter and getting to work on time. That apartment building was full of stories one after the other. I could hear another one of my neighbor getting beat by her man every other night. I was glad to be single, working and free.

Demons have their territories and the more you are aware of them the more you'll be able to recognize the type of demon forces in your area. The North side of Chicago had territorial demons that were off the chain. Sexual immorality was the biggest demon; lots of gays, prostitution, and all types of people really taken advantage of the old saying, "The Land Of The Free". It appeared to be more like the land of Sodom and Gomorrah; a place I read about in the Bible that was full of sexual immorality......

Recognize

Meet Renee

My life was starting to feel normal. I had a nice job, an apartment full of furniture, and my son was finally with me. Ajani was now six years old. The after-school program that kept him for free was the best thing that ever happened to me. The Cook County Court System never worked out for me, so I needed all the assistance I could get. The only downside was it was located in Cabrini Green. Cabrini Green was a very rough side of town. Lots of low income project buildings, which many of the tenants appeared to be in gangs or just were apart of that hard life. I wasn't afraid of the area, I just wasn't in the mood for drama. I also didn't want my son to have to fight with the roughnecks everyday. I know he was just six, but they start young these days. Besides, I hadn't shown him how to use a knife yet.

After picking my son up everyday for about two years, I became a regular and people started to accept me. I began to notice that most of the programs at the center were centered on the boys and it wasn't much for the girls to do. I decided to spend some of my free time as a volunteer at the center as a dance instructor. The director at the center thought that having a dance class was a good idea. He met with the staff, introduced me and told me when I could start.

My first day consisted of a tour of the entire center. I had no idea how large the center was, as I would just dart in and out just to pick up Ajani. He pointed out the bad kids, and he showed me where I would be conducting my dance classes. While we walked around the center, the director spoke to some of the kids, made some of the kids take off

Recognize

hats, and told others to go to the gym. As he looked at the doorway, we both saw a young girl, and he immediately said, "She is not allowed in the center." I looked at the girl and she looked at me. She was a little shorter than me, about five feet two inches, dark brown complexion. She had on jeans that were tattered and torn, a T-shirt from the center and an old pair of gym shoes. Her hair was very nappy and could have used a good washing, but she was pretty; nice teeth, a pretty shape, and smooth skin. As I looked at her I could tell that she was young, hard, but also soft. I needed to know why she wasn't allowed in the center. The director told her to leave. She looked at him and then me, rolled her eyes and left.

The guys at the center were fighting over who would take Ajani to the gym and look over him as I conducted my class. It was almost as if they were trying to fight for my hand in marriage. Everyone knew Ajani was my son, so they all kept an eye on him. I was unsure where to begin with my new dance class. The girls were starring at me and I them. They were dirty, dusty, nappy headed and loud, not to mention undisciplined and disrespectful. After a little time of dialogue, I realized that they were not sure of my age. After all, these teens were my size if not larger. I was 27 years old, five feet four inches and weighting 105 pounds. Many of these kids were a lot larger than me and this got me to thinking about doing something on nutrition.

"So what's your name?" one girl asked. "Toni", I replied. "Toni? That's a boys name," and they all started laughing. "Toni is a unisex name. It could be a girl or a boys name." "Unisex? That sounds gay!" another person said. "No, it's not the same as being gay. It only means that the name is kind of neutral and it could be used for either sex. My real name is Antoinette, but I prefer to be called Toni." One girl said, "I see why you like to be called Toni: Antoinette sounds like a white name. Are you from the suburbs?" "No. I'm from the Westside of Chicago," I said. "Well, you straight then. You cool people," one girl said.

After an hour of letting the girls get to know me and I them we ended the session with a "have a good night." They all laughed at me as if that was an impossible task. The funny thing about it, I knew why they were laughing, and I also knew that many of them wouldn't have a good night. "Tomorrow, we will get started with some simple modern dance steps so be ready," I said as they left the building. I went to the gym, got Ajani, and went home. As I walked to my car, I saw the girl with the tattered jeans in the crowd. She waited outside for the other girls to come out. I really wanted to know why she wasn't allowed in the center.

The next day, I went into my Director's office and asked. "Why is that girl not allowed in the Center?" "What girl? Who Renee! She is just bad news! I think she is in a gang!" he said. "The bottom line is she is not allowed in the Center!" "Okay," I said, "Let me make sure I understand what you are saying. She is in a gang, so she can't come into the Center. Isn't everyone around here in some type of gang?" "Well Toni," he said, "Renee feels that the rules don't apply to her. One of the rules is that you can't bring any weapons into the Center, and she carries a knife," he said. "How do you know?" I asked. He said, "Because I've seen it and the other kids have talked about it. I have enough trouble around here and I don't want to deal with her using her knife in my Center." "Do you know why she carries a knife? She could have a good reason," I said. "I just don't want to see her in

Recognize

the Center, and don't you get any bright ideas. I appreciate what you are doing with the girls here in the Center, but you can't help them all besides, shouldn't you be in your class now?" he said.

The girls were excited and the boys stood outside the door to see if they could sneak peeks at the girls in their dance attire. The funny part was when older young men would walk over as if to tell the little guys to get to the gym and stand there watching as well. I kept the door closed and put paper up over the glass part. This helped keep the spectators from standing outside the door. The girls were easy to teach. They were energetic, flexible, strong, and eager to learn. On the opposite side of the wall were windows leading out to the parking lot, but they were covered with mini- blinds. As I looked over at the windows, I could see someone looking in. It was Renee. I told the girls to close their eyes and feel the music. I told them that once they became one with the music, they could dance and keep up with every beat a lot better. As they completed this exercise, I went outside to talk to Renee. "Hi Renee," I said, "How do you know my name?" she asked. "I know a few things," I said. "Do you want to come to my dance class?" I asked. "Naw, I don't want to come to your stupid dance class." "Well, if my dance class is so stupid, why are you looking through the window at us?" "I can look wherever I want to," as she rolled her head. "Well, I believe it's because you can't dance, and you can't learn how to. You look like the type who would rather run from her problem than face them," I said, "so go ahead and just stand out here and watch us all night long." "I'm not running! That stupid man won't let me come in," she said. "What if I let you come in? Would you come?" "Yes," she said as she looked into the street. "Well, come on in," I said.

Renee walked with her head down and put her hands in her pockets and walked beside me. When we got into the class, most of the girls still had their eyes closed listening to the music. Renee just looked at them and then at me and asked, "What are they doing?" "I'll explain later," I said. I introduced Renee to the class, but they all knew her already, and many were glad to see her in class. As we ended the class and everyone left I asked Renee to wait a minute because I wanted to talk to her about the knife.

"I understand that the reason you are not allowed in the center is because you carry a knife." "Yeah!" she said. "Why? I asked. She put her head down and said, "I don't want no man to rape me. Girls get raped around here all the time even gang raped, and the police or nobody do nothing. I use my knife to keep those boys off me. They are always touching me. They touch my chest, and my butt and I don't like it. I don't want to be raped." I totally understood her. I know what it's like to have someone touch you that you don't want to have touch you. I really wanted to help Renee.

The next day Renee and I were entering the Center at the same time. The boys were in the doorway and wouldn't let Renee in. They were touching her behind and tugging at her jacket. I could hear her shout "Stop boy! You play too much! STOP!" The boys really didn't know how to deal with such a young girl who was built like a well-developed woman. As I approached the group, they all stood to the side to let me in, and Renee was already halfway down the hall. I could see the Director of the Center approach Renee and she pointed down in my direction. The Director asked to see me in his office. "I thought I asked you not to let that trouble maker in this center." "I don't think she is a troublemaker," I said. "I

Recognize

think someone needs to teach these over active teenage boys to keep their hands to themselves." After much dialogue about Renee, and reviewing how she was being treated by the boys, the Director decided to give her a chance in my dance class. He made it very clear that I would be responsible for any miss-behaving by Renee. It was a deal.

"Girls, are you ready to whip the pants off of the Boys and Girls Club? We are going to enter a citywide dance competition, and you have to be serious. I don't like working with a losing team." All of the girls were excited, including Renee. I was determined to give these girls a chance at being something and being a part of something good. Renee always wore the same clothes and had a body odor. I asked her about it and she told me some alarming stuff. She was the oldest of eight kids (she was only 13). She was practically raising these kids herself, and she lived in a Chicago Housing Authority (CHA) high rise that looked like a death trap. I asked her to let me meet her sisters and brothers, and her mother. I was curious to know where she lived. She took me to her apartment building and for the first time in my life I was face-to-face with a project highrise at night. Up close, it looked like an oversized monster from the pit of hell, with the smell of hell, and the darkness of hell. I asked Renee, "What floor do you live on?" She said the ninth floor. "How do we get there?" We could either wait on the elevator or take the stairs. "Which is safest?" I asked. She only looked. I took a deep breath, said a quick prayer and walked up nine flights of stairs in the dark. We stepped in urine, lazy dogs and dead mice. Over drunks, and other questionable people. I understood even better why Renee had her knife. I hated that I didn't have mine on me. I asked Renee, "Do you have your knife?" "Yes, I keep it on me at all times." Renee's house wasn't any better than the hall we just came from. It was dirty, empty and full of dirty little kids. All they had to eat was white bread, cheese and water from rusted pipes. "Where is your mother I asked?" "You'll meet her tomorrow," she said.

I couldn't sleep thinking about the conditions Renee and her sisters and brothers had to live in. I wanted to call someone. Maybe DCFS or maybe, well I couldn't think of anyone or any place. I just felt sad. I couldn't give Renee any of my clothes they would've been a size too little, but I did bring some soap, and other girly things she could use to spruce up a little. It was Friday, and I didn't teach on Friday. I went to the center to pick up Ajani, and saw Renee. "Do I get to meet your mother today?" I asked. "Yes. Let's go," she said.

We walked about one block and a half and along the way we saw an out-of-control woman in the middle of the street cursing and throwing glass bottles at the window of a liquor store. The owner was telling this woman not to come back, and she was just cursing and keeping up complete hell. She was small about five feet two inches and weighed about eighty-nine pounds. She did not have any teeth in her mouth, well, maybe one, but she looked like death on a stick. She reminded me of Mary from my father's liquor store. She was skinny, ugly, dirty, nasty and sick. She was what people in my neighborhood would call a crazy lady. Renee stopped to look at all of the commotion. I told her that I had to get home so we needed to hurry on to meet her mother. She said, "That's her right there." "Right where?" I asked. "Right there, the one throwing glass bottles at the store." We both stood there and watched her perform for about twenty

Recognize

minutes. A car rolled by and a voice shouted to Renee, "Get your crazy mama out the street!" Renee looked at me with guilt and shame. I didn't know what to say, I didn't know what to do.

Renee's mother spotted her, walked over and said, "Hey baby" while smiling. She looked funny with no teeth. "How my big girl doing," Renee said, "Fine. This is Toni." Her mother slowly turned to me while trying not to fall on her face. "Hi Toni, you shole is a pretty girl. You have to excuse me, I have to kick some a— around here," she said. All I could do was buck my eyes and say okay. Renee tried to get her mom to go home, but she was too out of control. I have always found it amazing how alcoholics could go in and out of different personalities. As Renee and I walked back toward the Center she explained that her mom was a good person when she wasn't drunk. She made me promise not to tell anyone that she and her sisters and brothers were always at home alone because she didn't want the system to arrest her mom and put them in shelters. I started to believe that the only good life I knew of was the ones on TV, like the Brady Bunch.

Time passed, things were under control, and the girls were really enjoying the dance classes. One day as I was entering the Center, I could see police lights near the center and I could sense that something was out of the norm. As I got near the Center, a police car blocked the entrance and told me that I couldn't go in. I told the cop that I had a son in the Center and I must get him, plus I needed to know what was going on. The cop asked me my name and as I told him, he went on his radio and said, "She's here!" My heart started to race and I really needed to know what was going on even more. Everyone was looking at me, and there was a crowd of people, the Director of the Center, lots of young people, and plenty of police standing near the door. As I got out of my car the stars became more intense. I was bracing myself for the worst, maybe my son is lost, maybe he got shot, maybe he's dead. I could see blood on the ground as I approached the front door. The Director walked over to me and yelled. "THIS IS ALL YOUR FAULT!!!" Renee stabbed a boy and now we have cops everywhere. Everyone emotions were a little high and I felt like I was in a scene from NYPD Blue. "Where did she stab the boy?" I asked. "Does it matter?" he asked. "Was the boy badly hurt, or was..." before I could finish the cop wanted to talk to me about Renee. I said, "Before I talk to anybody, I want to know what happened. Is there anyone out here that saw what happened?" There had to be 65 kids outside, someone had to know something. One of Renee's friends stepped up and said, "Well Renee was trying to get into the Center and the boys kept blocking her way. They were pulling on her breasts and rubbing on her butt, and one boy pulled her down to the ground and was jumping on her. Everybody started laughing and they all paid him a dollar. They were betting that he couldn't get none from Renee, but he won the bet. Renee was mad, and crying, and no one would help her. That boy kept messing with her even after he got his money. He put his leg out to trip her, and she cut his leg. That boy wasn't even hurt that bad. He was mad that Renee put a hole in his Levi's, so he tried to chase her and blood started coming out of his leg. I think Renee was hurt because she hit her head when they tripped her the first time, and it was five boys on top of her."

My focus immediately moved from the boy to Renee. I wanted to know where she was. They put her in a police

Recognize

wagon and took her to a local lock-up. I demanded to see her. I wanted to know if she was okay. As I walked to my car, a little old sickly looking woman approached me, "Please get my baby, please Miss. I don't know what I'll do if they take her from me." As I looked in the woman's face, I notice that this was Renee's Mom., whom I think was only about 35 years old. I told her that I would do everything I could to get her out of jail. I got in my car, put my head out of the window and asked a cop where could I find Renee? He pointed me in the right direction and off I went. I arrived at a nearby small brick building with blue steel doors. As I walked in, I saw two white male cops and one white female cop. "May I help you?" the woman cop asked. "Yes, I am here to see a girl named Renee. She was brought here about one hour ago." "Who are you?" she asked. "I'm her, her, her Aunt. Yes, I'm her Aunt." The cop looked at me as if I was lying, but still looked as if she was going to let me see her. "Have a seat," she said. After about two hours of just sitting, and watching the three cops do nothing, they finally told me to follow them. I went into some doors, around a corner to a small cell where Renee was sitting in the corner like a broken down rag doll. I waited until the cop left before I said anything to Renee. "Renee!" I said. She slowly looked around and as she saw that it was me, she ran to the bars and just held onto me through the bars. I just held her back. Although she didn't speak, and neither did I, we both said a lot. The floors were sticky. The place was nasty, and it had a strong smell of urine. I wanted to use all of my strength to bend the bars open and set her free. She just cried and cried and cried. I wanted to cry also, but I was too mad.

I didn't know what to do. I never knew anyone in jail. I didn't know how the system worked and I didn't know if I had to have money to get her out. So, I did what I knew to do when I don't know what to do, and that was to pray and ask God for help. I said, "Father God in the name of Jesus, help me get Renee out of jail. Please hear my prayer!" After what appeared to be an eternity Renee and I broke our embrace. I looked at her and she began to tell me what happened. "I didn't want to cut him, I didn't want to hurt anybody, I didn't want to come here. My sister and brothers are all alone." She continued to cry as she spoke. I told her that I know, I know, I know. That's all I could say. "I am going to try to get you out of here tonight." I said. I walked to the front and asked what do I need to do to get Renee out of jail. "She's a good girl and she doesn't belong here," I said to one of the cops. The woman cop looked at me while winking and said, "She can go now if an adult in her family were here. Will an Aunt do?" I asked hoping that the answer would be yes. "Yes!" the cop said. Getting her out took another two hours, but I was able to get her out and back to her apartment building.

Cabrini Green had its own demons operating in its territory; poverty, rape, control, and black-on-black crime. I'm reminded of one of my favorite scriptures found in 2 Chronicles:7:14 If my people who are called by My name will humble themselves, and pray and seek My face, and turn from their wicked ways, then I will hear from heaven, and will forgive their sins and heal their land.

Recognize

A PRAYER FOR EVERY PERSON BEHIND BARS

Father God I pray that You would move by your power right now in the mighty Name of Jesus. Touch every person reading this book who's behind bars right now. Deliver them as they read the words off of this page. For every innocent person and every ex-offender who is still suffering from the experience of being mistreated and locked up; I ask You right now Father God to break every yoke of bondage off of them right now. Break it off of their minds, their emotions, and stop the devil from ushering in bad memories recall and causing mental illness. Take every negative label off of them right now, and let them know that they belong to You. Father God let them know that You are able to forgive sin, restore character, and to speak to a dry place and give living waters. Lord I thank You for touching all of my sisters and brothers who are incarcerated and that You are bringing total healing to all parties involved, and are healing our land. By faith I seal this prayer In Jesus Christ's Name I pray! AMEN!

Meet Holiness

During my years of working, doing volunteer work, while being a single mom, I also wanted to live for Christ. I knew the Word; always have, but it didn't seem like I was doing what God wanted me to do. He kept snatching me out of the jaws of Satan over and over again that I decided that it must be some great work for me to do. The only problem that I had about living a totally clean life was that I had a boyfriend who didn't believe in all of that church stuff. His mom died when he was just a little boy and he had major issues with God and the church. I would try to teach him about God and teach him that God gives life, while Satan is the one who comes to steal, kill, and destroy. He didn't want to hear anything about God or the devil. All he knew was if God was so real, why would he take a good person like his mom off of the face of this earth? Some days it appeared as if he was coming around and other days, he didn't want to hear anything about God, the Bible or the church. The spirit of bitterness had set in and Satan was having a good time with him.

One day I went to a bible study and was so convicted about my relationship with my boyfriend that I decided to break it off with him and live strictly for God. I was already on the right track. I didn't drink, get high, hang out at clubs, so this salvation thing shouldn't be such a hard thing to do. All I needed to do was discuss my decision with my "man", hoping for his support. Part of me however knew that it would be a fight about me picking God over us. So, a good plan of action was to bring up God in some way knowing this would make him mad, and I could simply tell him that since I choose God and you seem to be so against God, why don't

Recognize

we go our separate ways. This plan sounded fault proof, but it backfired. He felt like God took his mother and now He was trying to take me from him. I didn't want to be manipulated to stay with him, but I didn't want to push him further away from God either. I didn't know what to do, so I just simply asked him not to see me for a while. I needed time to think and see what God wanted me to do.

We hadn't seen each other for weeks and this Sunday was Mothers Day. I really didn't like Mother's Day so much because my Mother and I were not as close as I would have liked and I hated being a single parent. I felt like life was unfair. But, after looking at my son with those big pretty eyes, I got over it. My boyfriend arrived at my front door dressed in his gym stuff (as usual) with a dozen roses and a nicely wrapped Mother's Day gift for me. I was surprised to see him. I knew Mothers Day was very hard for him not to mention that he and I hadn't spoken in days. It was good seeing him and I was so excited that he had brought me a gift. I loved getting gifts. It didn't even matter what was in the box. He handed me the roses and then the box. "You look wonderful," he said. "Thanks! I am on my way to church," I said. "Before you go to church, how about giving me some?" he said. I was so disgusted with the question that I just said, "I told you that I am on my way to church." He became indignant, snatched the roses and the box out of my hands, and told me to get a church boy because he was tired of being with me and not getting any. I was hurt and somewhat upset, but I tried to keep my composure. I was making a stand for God and I had to deal with everything that came with it. I headed to church with a very low spirit. It felt like living for God meant being without, being lonely, and being over-looked. In spite of my feelings, something inside of me was telling me to go ahead and live for God because only what you do for Him would last and because you are denying yourself for Him, He will take away the pain or give you the grace to endure.

Satan was always trying to destroy me and get me off my square with the spirit of rejection, but the more I found out that God was a healer and a deliverer, I began to get more spiritual muscles. I was not only learning the Word of God, but I was applying the word of God. I knew that I was more than a conqueror, and that my God was able to keep me from falling. I knew that the way Satan was after me that I needed to learn more of the Word of God, because without it I would perish. "The people perish for lack of knowledge became real in my life." I can remember many up front attacks that could have been avoided had I known how to rebuke, bind and loose. I was running to the church which is my first love to gain the knowledge that I needed to win this spiritual battle.

Recognize

Meet the Pastor's Son

Man, church was extra crowded. It was Mother's Day and everyone had on their Sunday best. My girlfriend Robin met me at church. It was good seeing her because she wasn't much of a church goer. She didn't like, nor understand the church world or the Word of God. I did my best to teach her what I knew, but the wall she had up was from years of hurt. Her mother abandoned her, her father, and the rest of her sisters and brothers to live the life of a street woman. Her mother and Renee's mother could pass for twins. They had the same demons operating in their lives. Robin was ashamed of her mother and she used to tell people that her mother was dead. My mother on the other hand, wasn't in the street. She was a homemaker, but was living a life of hurt, regret, and sorrow. As a result, Robin and I were at church on Mother's Day, but not really feeling the joyous effect that others seemed to be enjoying. As we stood along the walls trying not to get stepped on, Robin thanked me for inviting her out, but she didn't feel like standing during the service, and left. She promised me that she would return to church with me one day but never did. I felt somewhat like a failure. Here it is that I finally got Robin to come out to church and we couldn't get a seat. It could have been also that she wasn't feeling all of the Mother's Day stuff that was taking place. In a way I didn't blame her. I tried to keep my spirits up, because after all, I was a mother and I felt that my son deserved to have a mother with an upbeat spirit, and one who could show him some love.

The choir started to sing, and their voices seemed to

Recognize

bounce off the walls. It must have been about 150 choir members. They had great harmony, and appeared to really enjoy singing for the Lord. Just watching them sing with such energy began to lift my spirits. I started clapping my hands and stumping my feet. I was having a good time in the Lord.

It appeared that the choir was about to do another song. The Pastor said, "Today is Mother's Day, and I want Joseph to sing my Mother's favorite song!" The entire church went up in praise. I really didn't know what was going on or what was about to happen. But whatever was about to take place, the entire church was full of excitement. The music started and everyone began to stand up before the soloist took his position. I felt like shouting, "Sit down! I can't see! Sit down!" But I didn't of course. All of a sudden, a voice so sweet, so heavenly, so beautiful began to sing "WHY SHOULD I FEEL DISCOURAGED, AND WHY SHOULD THE SHADOWS FALL, AND WHY SHOULD MY HEART FEEL LONELY AND LONG FOR HEAVEN AND HOME? WHEN JESUS IS MY PORTION A CONSTANT FRIEND IS HE; FOR HIS EYE IS ON THE SPARROW AND I KNOW HE WATCHES ME. It felt like he took the word right from my soul and shared them with the entire church. I had never heard this song before, neither had I ever heard such a voice so beautiful. I had to see who was singing, because he was singing to me. I made my way through the crowd of people and stood at the front of the church so that I could just see who was singing. His eyes were closed for most of the song, but when he opened his eyes, he looked right into mine. I continued to look at him and he continued to look at me. It was almost as if the choir and all the other people in the church had disappeared and it was just him singing to me. The song was so beautiful that it brought tears to my eyes, but I didn't let them fall. This song was for every person in the place who didn't have a mother. Whose mother had gone on. It was for those who were mothers themselves, but were raising their children without the father. For every person in the place that needed to know that God's eye is on the sparrow, so you had to know that His eye was on you too. As he was bringing the song to a close, I made my way back to my spot against the wall in the back of the church. I felt like God was sending me a message through that song and that everything was going to be all right.

Church was over and everyone was making Mother Day plans. Everyone was walking around with their Mother's Day flowers, and just having a good time with what looked like generations of daughters, mother, and grandmothers. I watched different sets of people just wondering what type of plans they were making. In a sense I was wishing that my mother and I were together making plans. Anyway, I had to find Ajani. He loved running around the church.

"Is this who you're looking for?" It was the man who was singing that song, "Eye on the Sparrow." He had my son by the hand making a special delivery. I must admit that it was a pleasant surprise. "Yes. I was looking for this little guy. Where did you find him?" "Well put it like this, I know all the places that little kids like to hide around here." "Oh really?" "Yes," he said. "Well, thank you. Thank you very much." "Thank you too," he said. "And by the way what is your name?" he asked. "It's Toni. It's Toni with an "I"."

Recognize

"Hey Toni with an I." He made me laugh. "My name is Joseph, and that's Joseph with a "J"." He made me laugh again. I started feeling like a little high school girl. I was determined to hold back any additional laughter. "Well I better get going. I have Mother's Day stuff to attend to." "Where are you going, to your mother's house?" he asked. "No, I think I'm just going to eat out." "Great! Me too, let's go out together." "My treat since you are a mother, and I'm not." He did it again, he made me laugh. "Where would you like to go?" he asked. I really couldn't think of anything nice. I was use to eating Kentucky Fried Chicken, or Churches Chicken dinners every Sunday. "Oh, I know," I said. "Let's go to Bakers Square!" He looked at me with a big smirk on his face and said, "I think we can do better than that." "Okay, you decide" I said.

He was so excited and I really didn't know what was going on. I was excited that I didn't have to spend another Mother's Day eating Kentucky Fried Chicken. He pulled this big van around to the front of the church and told me to get in. I put my son in the back, put his seat belt on, and off we went. I didn't say much. I was just thinking, "This is a big van, and it looked like it cost a lot of money." It had a TV and VCR and all other kind of bells and whistles. Today was not the first time we'd seen each other. I've seen him around the church. I just didn't know he had such a beautiful voice. "What are you thinking about?" he asked. "Nothing really, I'm just chilling." "You know, I saw you starring at me today while I was singing." "I was not starring at you. I just wanted to see who was singing, and all of those people were in my way." "Well, I was singing to you," he said. "Yeah right! You didn't even know I was in the church. It was so crowded." "You would be amazed how much you can see from the choir stand," he said, "I knew you were coming to church, and I wanted you to hear me sing. So I asked my dad if I could sing on Mother's Day." "Who is your dad?" he laughed; "You don't know who my father is?" "No, I don't." "My father is the pastor," he said. "You are a PK?" "Yes, but I don't like to be called a PK." "No problem, I will call you Joseph with a "J" ," I said.

We were headed downtown. I had never eaten downtown. I could never afford to eat downtown, or should I say, by the time I paid for parking, I wouldn't have enough left to eat with. I was feeling a little uncomfortable. I was thinking, what if he runs out of money trying to impress me and the three of us end up washing dishes to pay for our meal? "Are we eating here?" I asked as I pointed to Lawrys Steak House. "Yes." He handed his keys to a man dressed like someone leading a parade and slipped him a few dollars. I thought to myself that this may be a beautiful ending to a day that started out so sour. As we waited to be seated, I looked all around and wondered how much this was going to cost, so I looked in my wallet to see how much cash I had on me just in case I needed to help out. "What are you doing?" he asked. "I'm just looking," before I could finish, he told me not to worry that he had everything under control. I was in shock. I had never been out with a man who had everything under control. I had always had to help out with the bill and we are talking Baker's Square. Don't get me wrong, I love Baker's Square. You can get a good meal and some great pie. As we sat down, I just did what everyone else was doing. I put my napkin in my lap and picked up my menu. There was nothing under $25. I told him that we didn't have to eat there, and

Recognize

he told me to relax, and said order whatever you want. I have my Dad's credit card.

I still didn't fully understand what was going on. I just felt like God was doing something wonderful for me since I took a strong stand for Him this morning. I was kind of missing Eric but was having too much fun and enjoying this new experience to let it effect me. "Are you enjoying your food?" he asked. "Yes! The food is great, but is it always this crowded?" "No, it's Mother's Day and all the restaurants are crowded today." We talked and really got to know a lot about each other. I found out that he had been hoping for a while that one day he and I could be really good friends. I was unsure about being with the pastor's son. After all, I had a son and many of the church mothers and some of the other deep Christians would look at me in judgment, and I didn't want to be put in the limelight. I liked the fact that the people didn't really know me. I didn't know if I had to live some type of "Mother Mary" type of life being with a PK or what. This relationship was the beginning of me growing up as a Christian. It was the beginning of more heartache, pain, determination, and courage also. It was the beginning of my recognizing who I was in God.

My mother was living in a courtway building during this time and the place caught on fire, and she had to move in with me. This was my mother's third fire. Joseph and I were enjoying a great friendship. He would never ring the doorbell. Instead he would stand outside my window and sing until I came to the window. My neighbors enjoyed hearing him sing. We would spend many of our Saturday's wedding hopping. Joseph would have anywhere from two to five weddings to sing at. He and I would decide the day of, which reception to attend based on the menu. We attended wedding, musicals, church anniversaries and other major church events. This was church at the max.

One Saturday Joseph and I attended about four weddings. As we arrived at these churches, they would rush him in as if he was the president of the United States. He would sing so beautifully, the people would be in awe, and we would rush out to the next wedding. The people would always try to get us to stay. Many of the wedding parties had space for us at the head tables, but we always had other weddings to attend. I would have never thought that church hopping and wedding hopping would be so much fun. One particular day, it was about 2pm now and we both were getting hungry. It was such a hot summer day, my hairdo had fallen and I didn't want to go back to any of the receptions. I really didn't feel like socializing. "Let's just go get a bite to eat," I said. "It'll have to be your treat, because I don't have any money," Joseph said. "You, don't have any money?! You just sang at four weddings! Didn't you get paid?" "No, Most of these people are my father's friends and associates, and I'm doing it for him." "You got to be kidding. You are buying gas, putting your best outfits in the cleaners, spending time learning songs that you don't know, and paying a musician. You don't work, so how are you making it? Do they at least pay your musician, or do you." "I do," said Joseph. "I don't get it. What do you plan to do to make a living for yourself?" "I never thought about it; My dad gives me money if I need it." I couldn't believe my ears.

A few weeks went by and my birthday was coming up.

Recognize

Joseph asked me my age and instead of answering his questions I told him to guess. He guessed that I was about 23. I was flattered because at the time I was 28. I told him that he should have known that I was older because I had a son who just turned seven. "Well, I didn't know what the deal was," he said. "How old are you?" "Guess," he said. "I don't know, I guess about 26." "NO, lower," he said. "Are you 23?" "No lower." "Don't tell me you're 19?" I said. "NO, higher," "20?" "Yes," he said. "20, you're only 20 years old, I CAN'T BELIEVE IT. I've been hanging out with a 20 year old. No wonder people have been looking at me crazy. No wonder I have so many player haters. I can't be with a 20 year old. What will your mother say? What will your father the Pastor say? What will my friends think? I am eight years older than you!!!! You are a baby." Needless to say, I was in shock. I couldn't believe that he was so young. It's wasn't proper for a woman to date a younger man. I had never heard of it. Plus in many ways he didn't appear that young. Maybe it was because he was raised in a better environment, had what I thought was a loving family, and had experienced some finer things in life. I didn't know if I could handle the pressure of dating a PK that was 8 years younger than me.

Joseph called me the next morning, and I told my mother to tell him that I wasn't there. This went on for about four days. My mother asked me what was up with me and Joseph. Why doesn't he come over anymore? She missed his singing, and why was I telling her to tell that I wasn't there. I told her the horrible news that he was 8 years younger than me. She laughed and told me that men do it all the time. If I liked him and he liked me what difference did it make? She reminded me how much fun I had with him every weekend before I knew his age and for me to get over it. She told me that she wasn't going to tell him that I wasn't at home anymore, and that the next time he called, she was going to give me the phone.

My mother walked into my room with the phone in her hand. "It's Joseph," she whispered. I took a deep breath, and said "Hello." "Hey, my mother wants to speak to you." "Wait, wait and don't put your mother on the phone! What does she want to talk to me about?" "Well, I told her about me and you and she wants you to know that she is okay with us being together, and she feels that if she is okay with it then I shouldn't care about what other people think." "Well, does she know my age?" "Yes." "Well, does she know that I have a son?" "Yes." "Well, okay put her on the phone." The voice on the other end said, "Toni." "Yes." "How are you?" "Fine." "Well I just wanted to let you know that my son has explained everything to me, and he really loves you, and if he loves you then I love you, and you have my blessings to date him if you'd like. Don't worry about what the people are going to say. Church folk will talk about you no matter how you slice the pie, so just enjoy your life; and don't you worry about the pastor, I will handle him. So here's Joseph." "Thank you," I said.

"I'm tripping, I can't believe that you put your mother on the phone. Y'all are like the Brady Bunch or something. What's up with your mother giving me permission to date you?" "Well you told me that you were concerned about what the people were going to say, and I felt like the only people you should have been concerned about were my parents, and now that they have accepted you, you shouldn't have a problem with us being together." It was a little weird, but he had a point. He came over and my son was really glad to see

Recognize

him, and so was I. "Hey, old lady," he said. "Hey, little boy," I said, and we both laughed. After we got past the age thing, everything was back to normal, whatever normal was. He had more upcoming weddings to sing at and wanted me to hear some of the stuff. He had such a great voice that he could sing to me anytime.

The news got out that Joseph and I were dating. Girls would roll their eyes at me. The older women in the church told me that I should be ashamed of myself. One woman even told me that she was grooming her daughter for the pastor's son and that I ruined all of her plans and that she hated me. The name calling got worse. People would find my name and number on the church phone list, call me up and call me all kinds of desperate whores and bitches and hang up the phone. People in the church would ask me if I was dating Joseph because there was a shortage of men and I was too old to get one my own age. The attacks were fierce and continual. Even some of the men would say to me, "When you are ready for a real man let me know." I would attend banquets with Joseph where he was the keynote entertainer, and they would put him at the VIP table and would try to put me at any second hand empty table. Joseph would see to it that they would put me at the table with him anytime we were together. When it was time for him to sing, he would get up and leave me at the table with a group of bitter and curious people that spent most of the time asking me questions about Joseph and I. Is it true that you are 10 years older than Joseph? Is it true that you have a child Joseph's age? Are you with him for his money, or because you know that he will be rich and famous one day? Who are your parents? Are they pastors? What do you do for a living? Or are you just a money chaser? The fun that I once shared with Joseph was turning into a nightmare. The funny thing about it all, is that, I was doing more for Joseph than he was doing for me. He didn't have any money until I started managing his affairs. People were more concerned about rumors, and using hurtful words, than my soul's salvation. I felt like you needed to really know who you were in God before interacting with the church folk. They were meaner than a thief in the street. I had more fights in the church than in the streets. This would have been a great place to apply the full armor of God had I known how to apply it.

Recognize

Meet Joseph's Manager

One morning Joseph called me with some great news. A well known gospel group wanted him to be a lead singer on their next album, and they wanted to speak to his manager. He wanted to know what he should do. I told him that I could make like I was his manager. He didn't think that that was a good idea because these people were also good friends with his dad, and they would tell his dad about me being his manager. Joseph's dad told him to be careful with me, that I was just looking for someone to help me take care of my son. He wanted his son to enjoy himself with me, but didn't want me to take advantage of him. I felt that his father and friends were taking advantage of him. They would have him all over the city singing and wouldn't pay him a dime, not even give him a love offering. We had to change my name. My business name was Marie Miller. So anytime someone would call my house looking for Marie Miller I knew that they were interested in booking Joseph for an event. Joseph's career really started to take off, and he enjoyed getting paid for his talent. He would always tell me, "Even if you and I don't make it, I'll never forget about you. I'll never forget how you helped me and were always there for me." I told Joseph all I would want from you was for him to sing at my wedding for no charge. I loved his voice so much, and knew that God would take him so far, that I didn't want him to get so big that he'd be unaffordable by the time I got married. I knew in my heart that Joseph and I wouldn't be together forever. That it was only for a season.

"May I speak to Marie Miller?" The voice on the other end asked. "This is she. How can I help you? This is T from

Recognize

Detroit and we wanted to know how much it would cost us to have Joseph fly into town for four nights and sing on our next family and friends CD?" I was so shocked to be on the phone with this well-known person, that I had to put him on hold and think about it. I hadn't put together a price list yet. So, after about five minutes, I told him that they would have to pay for two plane tickets, hotel for four nights, and $500 for each song that they wanted him to sing, plus cover all food expenses. They were okay with everything except the two plane tickets. They mailed the contract, and all was well. Joseph went to Detroit and when he got there, they didn't have any hotel accommodations for him, and he ended up sleeping on the floor at one of the artist house. He was okay with it, but I wasn't. I wanted to be aggressive with the language in the contract, but he told me not to worry about it. He was having fun kicking it with so many well-known recording artist, and plus he didn't want his dad to get wind that his infamous manager was strong arming folk.

Joseph and I spent a lot of time together. From church, to wedding, to the gospel fest, to just chilling at my apartment. Joseph also had a very sick uncle who spent his last days in the hospital. Joseph and I would sneak him soul food because he hated the hospital food, and Joseph would entertain the nurses with a few songs. There were also days when his dad would call me and ask me to send his son home. The funny thing about all of this was that we weren't doing the sex thing. Joseph was very loving, sensitive, and full of compassion. He enjoyed my son and was free from the trials of life. I made sure not to clue him in on all the hell that I had experienced until one day he asked me "DO I SEE THAT?" "See what?" "Look, over there by the wall. Keep looking and you are going to see a demon." At first I thought he was just joking around, but he wasn't. He said it again, "Look, there it is. He is looking around the corner at us." "I don't see it," I said. What does it look like?" "It's about three feet tall, kind of fat, and has knots all over his body." Why do you think he's here?" I asked. "I don't know, but he's afraid of us." I asked Joseph if this was the first time he'd ever seen a demon and he said no. "I see them all the time, but I haven't told anyone until now, because I don't want people to think that I'm crazy. I trust you and I know that you would believe me, and that you wouldn't laugh at me, or think that I was crazy." It was hard to believe, but he was so serious, that I had to trust that he was telling the truth. I told Joseph to tell me anytime he saw a demon, to describe it and to tell me what he thought the demon was up to.

One day we walked into a church. It was the church's anniversary. When we got up to the door, Joseph couldn't go in because he said that there were too many demons in there. As his manager, I had to tell the people that Joseph wasn't feeling well and that he wouldn't be singing today. He said, "You didn't see them? They were all over the place." I would ask Joseph questions like, "Why do you think they're here, or why do you think that you can see them and other people can't?" He would always say, "If you pay attention you will be able to see them too." After a while I was able to spot demons in people, but never really able to see a demon in full images. Joseph discovered that the demons were afraid of me, and that they didn't bother him when he was with me, but when he was alone, sometimes they would show up and stick around longer. They would give him headaches.

On another occasion, Joseph and I were going to a big

event where he had to sing. I picked him up and had on a nice sun dress. His mother asked me if I had planned on wearing that to the event. I said yes. Joseph was cleaner than the board of health, and I knew that I was under-dressed compared to his attire. She went into her closet and tried to find something more suitable that would fit me. She had an old suit that fit and let me borrow some jewelry. I felt really pretty, and more like an upper class lady. I had on earrings with the necklace to match. I kept touching my neck all night to make sure that the necklace was still there. When we arrived, the church was crowded. I wasn't worried because I knew that we had reserved seats up in the front. I sat by an elderly woman who kept looking at me, while Joseph sat in the VIP section with the pastors and other event guess. We did sign language to each other all throughout the event. He was trying to tell me that he was nervous, and I was trying to tell him to just relax, that everything was going to be alright. We were to far away from each other for me to ask him if he saw any demons, so I just prayed for him and prayed against any demons.

"Are you with that singer from Chicago?" "Yes mama. Well, do you know that he can see demons?" I looked at her and wondered how did she know that he could see demons. "Yes, I know, but how do you know?" I asked. All she said was, "Like people know like people." I believe that she was a prophet, because next she told me to stick by him no matter what, and stop letting the people hurt my heart. She told me to cover my heart more, and to just enjoy life until this road was over, and to not let bitterness take up residency with me. I couldn't get these words out of my mind. Joseph was up singing and the place was going crazy. People were shouting, clapping, and running around the sanctuary. The elderly lady and I continued to talk, and she asked me question after question. "How do you feel when he's up singing? Do you know that you bring him strength? Do you know that you have the power to destroy demonic activities?" You're not with him to be his girlfriend. The picture is much bigger. Pray and ask God to show you the big picture and be blessed. The music was loud, and there was so much stuff going on that it was almost as if this woman had disappeared into thin air. The altar was full of repenting people; I was on the front row and was trying to get out of the way, while at the same time looking for the woman who seemed to be full of wisdom, knowledge and spiritual insight. But she was nowhere to be found. She was gone.

Joseph asked me how he did. I told him that he did fine, but my mind was really off into space. I was trying to get the full jist of what I had just been told. Joseph and I stayed around, and he made his rounds, shaking hands, hugging, and giving out his contact information for other possible singing engagements. There was food in the basement. We ate, and got back on the road to go home. Joseph asked me what were me and Elder Smith talking about. He added, "You know that that was the pastor's mother?" "No, I didn't know." Yeah, she is a very powerful evangelist, and she must really like you, because you all talked all night." "Yeah she was giving me words of wisdom." Joseph said, "Well that woman is pretty deep, she is so deep that she can lay her hands on you and you would faint." Joseph was so dramatic at times that all I could do was laugh when he would say stuff like that. But on the other hand, I did find her to be a bit deep. Joseph knew everybody. He knew who was who, who was whom daughter, son, husband, wife, who had money, and who was cheating on whom. He had all the details on the

Recognize

church folk from near and far. And everywhere I went whether with Joseph or not, people started knowing me as Joseph's girlfriend.

Big things were starting to happen for Joseph. More and more singing engagements, the possibility of a one million dollar record deal, more and more women were making offers to him. His life was really taking off. I needed to re-look at what I wanted out of my life, and to make sure I was putting certain building blocks in place for my son. I didn't want people to think that I was just waiting around for Joseph big record deal, so I tried to limit the amount of time that I spent with Joseph. I knew we weren't going to be together forever. I just needed to know that he would be okay. One day I told Joseph that we needed to give each other some space. He took this as a break up. He cried all night, and different people in his family called me to find out why I was being this way toward Joseph. His sister-in-law called me to tell me that they found him in a nearby park crying and talking about killing himself, but they talked with him, let him express his feelings and after hours of discussion, he was okay. She really wanted me to stay with him and not worry about the small stuff, that everything would work out. She also warned me to be expecting a call from the first lady.

It was Sunday again, and Joseph was about to sing. The church was so ready to hear him that they were already on their feet. I usually stood as well, but sometimes I didn't. It was difficult for me to know how to behave in church because everyone was always looking at me. He started out with a testimony. "Before I sing, I just want to talk to those who may be going through something," he said. He continued with, "You know life can be hard and the trials of life can get you down, but just know that God is with you." "Amen brother," some people had replied. "But if God's eye can be on a little bitty sparrow then His eye is on you. His eye is on your relationship, on your finances, and on your situation no matter what it is." He went on and on. As he was testifying, his sister-in-law looked at me from the choir stand and just shook her head. As he was singing, he got halfway through the song, threw down the mic, and dashed behind the choir-stand. His mother, brother and aunt dashed after him. I just sat there wondering if I should go and see about him as well. I casually got up and walked behind the choir-stand. As I stood at the door, I could hear his mother reprimanding him saying. "You better not embarrass this family anymore, get yourself together. If Toni's not the one, there are plenty of other girls that would love to be with you and be apart of this family. You get yourself together." She realized that I was standing there after the fact and just walked away. I looked at Joseph and asked him what was that all about. He started to tell me about his mother, but I was referring to the outburst in church. We left the church so we could talk in private.

Joseph and I had a very good long conversation. He shared some deep family secrets with me, and I shared something's about me. He cried a lot and wondered why I never cried. I told him that it really wasn't cool to cry about where I came from, and it took too much energy. We went downtown to Bennigan's to get something to eat and the Sunday crowd beat us, so we had to wait for about one hour to eat. As we waited he asked me a question. He said, "Toni, since you don't cry about anything, because it's not cool to cry, tell me about sometime when you wanted to cry and just didn't." I really didn't want to do that, and really didn't know why I didn't. "Nah. Maybe later." "What's wrong with now?

Recognize

We have one hour to kill." "Okay, okay, I remember a time when I was sleeping in a car, and it was cold, and another time when I didn't have food to eat, and another time, when I didn't have money to go to school, and another time when I was performing and no one was there to cheer me on, and another time when I was in the hospital and got no visitors. My list went on and on, and all of a sudden, a river of tears fell down my face, and they wouldn't stop. I cried for hours, and hours. I made up for lost time I guess. I didn't know that my body had that much water in it. Joseph cried too. All he could say was I'm sorry this world was so mean to you. I'm sorry." I cried so hard that I could not even eat dinner. He said to me, "When you cry, I cry."

After Joseph realized that I had had such an interesting background, he wanted to be to me what I was to him a blessing. He would write me songs, go out of his way to show me how special I was to him, and he made a promise and swore that no man or woman could ever break it, no matter what. He said, I know you don't want anything from me, and I know you love me for who I am and not because I'm a PK or because I can sing. I promise you that when I get my record deal I'm going to take care of you and Ajani, even if I'm married to someone else." It was a cute promise, but I knew that no woman in her right mind would let her husband support another woman, but because it was such a genuine promise, I just said okay. Time went on. I helped and supported him financially so that he could get into the studio to lay his music and stuff. We continued to church hop and make our way around the city. Me and his mother spent time at women conferences, local church events, and all was well. Joseph would reinforce his promise by singing a song to me that was written by Baby Face. He would sing it on a regular basis. It was called "Give It A Chance." The lyrics were so befitting, and so him, that I lived and almost died by the words of that song. Some of the lyrics were, "YOU'RE NOT ALONE GIRL, AND NO ONE GONNA HURT YOUR HEART AGAIN, ERASE THAT THOUGHT, YOU'RE SO BEAUTIFUL PLEASE STAY THE WAY YOU ARE; KNOW ONE KNOWS THE PAIN THAT YOU'VE BEEN THROUGH, THEY TOOK THE BEST FROM YOU. GIRL I KNOW, YOU GAVE IT ALL YOU GOT, DON'T CRY IT'S OVER NOW, DON'T SIGH THINKS ARE BETTER NOW, I WILL GIVE YOU EVERYTHING YOU NEED YOU CAN ALWAYS COUNT ON ME GIRL "GIVE IT A CHANCE", I'LL MAKE IT UP TO YOU, GIRL GIVE IT A CHANCE, I'LL PROVE THIS WORLD WAS WRONG GIRL GIVE IT A CHANGE, I'LL MAKE IT UP TO YOU, I'LL TEACH THIS WORLD A LESSON AND NEVER, NEVER, NEVER LET YOU FALL. I found myself humming these lyrics all the time. These words brought me hope.

It's time for Joseph's big début concert. I worked like a dog for this event. I paid for much of his studio time so that he could get demo tracks out to the record companies. I did his biography, flyers, and other mailers. I really wanted this to be his big day. He was excited and I was excited for him. Many well-known gospel artists were there and things were looking up for Joseph. At the end of the day, there were so many people in his dressing room that I could hardly get in to tell him what a great job he did. He barely noticed me, but I just figured that he was really excited and busy trying to interact with his fans until he looked up at me and said, "Don't you need to get Ajani in the bed? It's pretty late, you

Recognize

should go home." He'd never been concerned in the past about what time I put my son to bed. The excitement was changing things a bit. I just stood back, watched from a distance, and knew that things were changing. I went home and figured he could fill me in on things in the morning. My girlfriends called me the next morning just to tell me how many women were giving Joseph their phone numbers and pushing up on him. They enjoyed giving me such negative reports. I learned to guard my heart just like the woman told me to, and worked hard not to buy into bitterness.

One day Joseph asked me did I remember that time when I told him that we needed a little time and space away from each other. "Yes, I remember. I believe that was about one and a half years ago," I said. "Yeah, but I think you were right. We do need some time away from each other," he said. I asked him when he wanted to start with the space. He said ASAP! By this time he had already been out on dates with his new girlfriend. He was seen with her at our favorite restaurant several times already. It appeared that everyone in the church knew about this new girl except me. I would call Joseph, and he wasn't at home. Some Sundays he wouldn't be at church. When I walked in the ladies room people would turn, look at me and would smirk as they walked away. It was as if I had awakened and found myself in the twilight zone. I finally got an opportunity to ask Joseph if he was seeing anyone else and he told me that he had a few friends, but it wasn't anything serious.

It was our choir anniversary and by this time I was in the choir. As I looked out into the audience I couldn't help but notice these two white girls. They both were pretty and really seemed to know quite a few people in the church. I was wondering why I didn't know who they were. When church was over, everyone was planning to get a late-night snack as we always did. At this point I really didn't have anyone to hang with, because my hanging buddy was busy introducing his new white girlfriend to people. Everyone was making a big fuss over this girl. Joseph's sister-in-law came over to me to see if I was okay. She said, "Joseph asked me to take you out of the church because he was feeling funny with you watching him. He's afraid that you are going to make a scene." I was shocked because Joseph knew that that wasn't my style. I just said, "Ask Joseph is he going to introduce me to his new girlfriend." She came back and said that it would be best that I left because everyone is looking at me like I was the fool. My life was changing. Life as I knew it for the last four years was coming to an end. It sneaked up on me before I was ready for it. I went home, laid in my bed, and wondered how many people were laughing and talking about me behind my back.

Recognize

Meet the First Lady

Months had passed and now it was time for the Pastor's anniversary. The pastor knew some of the greatest gospel artists. Shirley Caesar, The Tommies, The Winans, and the list went on and on. For the last four years, I sat right next to the first lady. The funny thing about "my seat" was that I sat next to her before knowing that she was Joseph's mother. I liked sitting next to her. I thought she was pretty, classy, and always smelled good. I often wondered if my own mother smelled this good because I don't ever remember getting close enough to her to know. I would always say to myself, one day I'm going to buy myself some perfume so that I could smell like an important lady. Every now and then I would lean over just to smell her perfume. I thought to myself that even though Joseph and I were over, I still had a pretty good relationship with his mom. She and I would go to women's conferences together, sit in her kitchen and talk, while she cooked, and spend time out at dinner. We would even talk about what it was like being a first lady and having so many people hate you in the church. I really enjoyed learning how to be a lady from her coaching me. But, I also knew that she needed a friend and someone she could trust. Our friendship outside of my relationship with her son, was pretty strong I thought.

I had a feeling that people from all over the city would be at this big gala, so, I was stressing over what to wear. The news was out about Joseph's new girlfriend and his old jealous one. I couldn't escape the drama. After much thinking, I decided to stay home. I got a phone call from one of my girlfriends asking me what time did I think I would make it

Recognize

to the church. I said that I wasn't going. "You have to go. If you don't you know the church folk are going to talk about you. They are going to say, you are depressed, or were too jealous to show your face. You have to come even if you don't stay long." "Okay, okay, I'll be there." As I arrived at the church, there were cars everywhere. People were pointing at me, and as I imagine talking about how I'm the ex-girlfriend that's been dumped for a white girl. I walked in the church heading to the sanctuary, Joseph's sister-in-law caught me before I went in to warn me of a few things. We rushed to the ladies room for a little privacy. "Girl, I'm glad I caught you! Your normal seat is taken. Joseph's new girlfriend is sitting right next to Sister Caldwell (Joseph's mother), and there are no more seats available. People are waiting for you to walk in so that they can see the look on your face, so I'm warning you of what's going on. Some people are making bets that you are going to lose it. I don't know what you gonna do girl, but walk in with your head up, and don't look shocked when you see her sitting with Sister Caldwell. She has her entire family with her, and the pastor is going to give them some type of big acknowledgment because her father's church made some type of big donation. He has his own church, and I found out that she is a PK too. They are making a big deal over this girl and her family because she comes from money. So girl get ready." This is going to be a night full of lots of drama." She had to leave and get back in the choirstand as they were about to sing a song. The choir always kicked off the Pastor's anniversary with some grand opening number.

I walked around the side door to get a peek inside the sanctuary. I needed to see where all the players were, in terms of the new girl friend and her family. Someone behind me said, "Are you going in or not?" so I was in the sanctuary before I was ready to be. The choir director was so involved with the whole let's wait for Toni to walk in plot, that he could not pay attention to what he was doing, so as a result, the entire church was silent when I walked in. I walked over to Sister Caldwell and kissed her like I always did, spoke to her guest, waved at all the familiar faces and stood against the nearest wall to enjoy the sound of the choir. I had a smile on my face that was plastered there from nervousness, shame and disappointment. I didn't like the fact that people were waiting for me to walk in just to see how I would handle myself. Where were my friends? On the other hand, I thank God that Joseph's sister-in-law had enough love for me to help soften my blow. I sang, clapped and said Amen in all the right places, but I was waiting for this night to be over. I spotted one of my girlfriends, and she made room for me right behind Sister Caldwell.

All of us had to sit there and deal with this awkward situation. It almost felt like they were just as uncomfortable as I was. Maybe it was because of the way I was being treated by them and not showing any animosity. The church program was almost over and I went out into the hallway just to get a little air. People were all buzzing about Joseph's record deal. It appeared that Joseph just landed a one million dollar record deal. I was very disappointed that he didn't tell me, especially since I spent quite a bit of money helping him make it all happen. I overheard someone say, "Did you see Joseph's girlfriend's new fur coat? He brought her that coat right after he found out about his record deal. Too bad for Toni." The crowd saw me standing there and just turned their heads. There was a lot of hype about Joseph's record deal, but I was waiting to hear the news from him.

Recognize

The phone rang and it was Joseph, "I just wanted to tell you about my record deal. I will probably be leaving for LA soon, but my debut party is next week and you are welcome to attend." I was glad to hear that. I figured he would use that opportunity to thank me for helping him along the way. His event was at some club downtown. Many of the church folk were there, along with Sister Caldwell and her new running buddy (Joseph's new girlfriend). He sang songs from his new album, signed autographed pictures, and spent a huge amount of time introducing his new girl to his producers. One of my girlfriends asked me if I was okay. "Y'all, I'm just waiting to see if he is going to at least thank me for all of my hard work and financial contributions." In addition, I couldn't help but wonder where he got the song, "When You Cry, I Cry." This song was being played all over the country.

His producer and project manager wanted to make some special acknowledgements. They thanked God, his parents, his investors and named them all by name, but my name wasn't ever mentioned. Even more of a surprise to me was to learn that there were women in the church who were funding his project. Last but not least his new woman. She was in the spotlight waving as if she has just won the Miss America crown. I can support mixed couples dating, I guess, but I couldn't help but wonder, do broke brothers like dating black women and when they make it big feel that part of their success is dating a white one? Who really knows. I tried to endure for a few more minutes prior to making my way to the front door. One of his musicians saw me on my way out, and wanted to know if he could call me later. "Sure, why not," I said. Anything to get out of the door. I made it home and couldn't stop kicking myself for putting myself in the ungodly environment. I was just walking into one tormenting situation after another.

The following months were full of radio interviews, TV videos, and phone calls from people keeping me in the loop of Joseph's affairs. I couldn't believe that our friendship had become so meaningless to him. It was time for another women's conference. I enjoyed learning about the things of God and couldn't continue to sit around waiting for Sister Caldwell to invite me out with her as she would in the past. So, I got me a ticket and went downtown to a huge women conference. As I went into the ladies room to freshen up my lipstick to my surprise I saw Sister Caldwell. I was really glad to see her. She was sharp as usual and pretty cordial. I wanted to know where she was sitting so maybe we could sit together like old times. Then her new running buddy came from out of the stall, and that changed things a little. I spoke and walked out the bathroom. It was clear to me that when I was dating Joseph, I was dating the entire family, and when it was over, the entire family was done with me as well. I couldn't escape my darkness. My entire life was church and a large part of me was attached to that church. I couldn't separate my love for God from the people of the church, and my wounds looked like they would never heal.

Joseph and my son still, however, had a very special relationship. He still would pick him up and let him hang out with him and his new girl. After a while, this wore thin, and he told my ten year old that he could no longer hang out with him. My son cried for hours. I called to ask Joseph about his decision and wanted to know why he didn't tell me about it first so that I could make it easier on my son. Sister Caldwell answered the phone after I had called there about five times, and asked me what is it that I wanted. "Well, I

Recognize

need to talk to Joseph to see why he dumped my son," I said. My son is over here crying his head off, and I just want to know what it is that Joseph said to him." She began to read me my rights. She said, "My son doesn't owe you anything. He doesn't want you and you need to get on with your life. He has someone in his life and you need to get someone in yours. Your son is not his son, and he doesn't have to do anything for that boy. My son doesn't have any kids and anything that he's done for that boy was out of the kindness of his heart, so quit calling here." Her outburst left me feeling worse, disappointed and depressed. I was not trying to make any enemies or have this be the next Sunday's topic for pastor. I just tried to comfort my son and ask God why do I have to continue to be hurt by people. Not just people in the street, but people in the church as well. I was in a very dry place but still had so much love for God that I couldn't give up.

After months of trying to recover from that last episode, the entire church was preparing for the annual holy convorcation held in Memphis, Tennessee every year. This was going to be my first year of attendance. All the other years I wasn't able to afford the trip. This trip was full of nightly gospel concerts, spiritual workshops and other events such as plays and just plain old fellowship. When I and my two girlfriends arrived at the hotel, we unpacked and reviewed the conference package to see which events we wanted to attend. As we reviewed our package, we noticed that Joseph was going to be in town starring in a well advertised gospel play. The opening night was right there in Memphis. "Hey, Toni, you think Joseph can get us some tickets?" "I doubt it. He's big time now, and he ain't trying to do anything for anybody." But if we see him, I'll ask." We got settled in, and decided to go out and get a bite to eat.

Wouldn't you know it, we saw the big superstar Joseph. After seeing him I didn't feel in my spirit that it would be a good idea to ask him for free tickets, but I didn't stop my girls from asking. Just as I thought, he explained that he could only give out so many tickets per show, and he had given out his limit. The folks were talking about how great the play was so I had to see it for myself. I didn't see Joseph anymore while I was in Memphis, so I called his home back in Chicago to see if his mother would give me his hotel phone number so I could give him feedback on the play. In the past, Joseph really loved getting feedback from me. His mother made it very clear that it wouldn't be a good idea for me to have his phone number. I don't know why I was shocked that she wouldn't give me the number.

The conference was over and it was time for everyone to go back to their hometown. It was a bittersweet vacation for me but overall good. I had more church than I could stand. Church in the morning, church in the evening, and church all night long. People had negative and positive things to say about Joseph's role in the play, but I had no way of forwarding this feedback to him. I made it back home and about three weeks later, I got a phone call from someone very close to the Caldwell family telling me that Joseph was still in Memphis and was trying to commit suicide. I was told that his family has had some of the biggest and the baddest evangelists and pastors from all over the world praying for him but he wasn't getting any better. People were starting to talk and were saying that Joseph was going crazy and that he must be doing drugs because he was claiming to see demons. His job with the production was at risk because of his mental state.

Recognize

The phone rang and it was his mother. "Toni, I need you to do me a favor. Joseph is in Memphis, talking about demons are trying to make him jump out the window. I need you to talk to him." "I don't have a number for Joseph," I said. "I know you don't, but I will give you his number. Can you please call and talk to him. I believe that you are the only one who may be able to talk some sense into him." I was thinking how his number was off limits just three weeks prior, but now I was asked to call him. "I will call him, and just for the record, Joseph is not crazy. He really does see demons." I dialed Joseph number in Memphis and heard a voice of a child answering the phone. "Joseph," I said, "Yes, who is this?" "This is Toni. What's up with you?" "I keep hearing voices in my head," he said. I spoke to him with authority. I said, "The devil is a liar! He cannot have you! You are a child of God and he better get his filthy hands off you. You better speak to every demon that tries to attack you and tell them to leave you alone. I remember you telling me that when you sing the demons run. So sing, sing to the glory of God. Sing, sing! As a matter of fact sing something right now," I commanded. He sang about 3 songs, and the spirit of the LORD filled his hotel room and the old Joseph was back. I thank God that bitterness, and rejection did not stop me from being used by God in his life. I knew that God was teaching me that my gifts were for His glory and for the body of Christ and not for any other purpose. I never heard from Joseph after this. I only heard that he was doing well, married with a baby on the way.

We need to recognize that Satan will use every tactic that He can to separate us from the Love of God. I believe since he was unable to get me out in the street, he tried to destroy me with the very thing that I always loved and that was the church. I took a few blows to the head, heart, and emotions, but as I prayed for myself and laid hands on myself. God gave me the victory. Many of the battles that I fought were not my battles. I now know that I'm just a vessel used of God and none of these battles are mine, but the Lords. I know who I am in God. I know that my God did not give me fear, but faith; therefore I don't fear Satan or his team of demons, but by faith I operate in the Power of the Holy Spirit, led by my daddy God and my Lord and Savior Jesus Christ.

Recognize

Meet Voo Doo

In the midst of all that was going on in my life, I knew that God was with me. By now I had a wonderful job working for a big phone company as a Customer Service Supervisor. I had a nice apartment in the suburbs, and God blessed me with a pretty nice car. I felt like I had gone from rags to riches, all without selling my body, drugs, or getting child support.

I saw the Magic Man at my brother's wedding. He was looking good, feeling good, and we all had fun dancing together on the dance floor. The night was getting long and he was about to leave. "Where are you going daddy?" I asked. He said, "Well I'm going to get me a little rest. I haven't been feeling good lately and I have to go to the doctor on Monday," he said as he kept walking. I kept pace with him and wanted to know what was up. I had never known my father to be sick or ever visit a doctor. He would always say "a little wine a day will keep the doctor away." But this time he explained that it was hard for him to swallow and he was just going to get things checked out. "Cool," I said. "Call me and let me know what the doctor says." "No problem," he said as he got into his car.

I ran back to the wedding party and told my sisters that daddy was going to the doctor and he looked worried. " I hoped everything was alright," I said. Everyone looked concerned but kept on interacting at the wedding. As I sat there looking at the people, I wondered if I would ever get married, and what was it that I really wanted to do with my life. I also thought about the look in the Magic Man's eyes

Recognize

when he told me he wasn't feeling well.

It was time to go home. The party was over and everyone was kissing the bride and shaking hands with the groom. I had a long way home and enjoyed just listening to the sounds coming from my radio. Time passed and weeks later I heard from the Magic Man. He told me that he had to have surgery because he had a tumor behind his throat and the doctors needed to cut it out so he could eat and swallow better.

During this time I was thinking about going to beauty school. It was a time where many people were being laid off and finding themselves homeless. I didn't want to end up in the streets again and wanted to find something I could do to bring in a little cash in case of an emergency. I checked around and found out that school was expensive and the hours were long, but I also thought about how unemployment left so many people without hope, especially people like me who made too much money for assistance and not enough to live 'the good life.'

After much praying and planning, I decided to get a roommate and go to beauty school. God was so good that he set it up where I could attend school while still being on the clock at my job. He allowed me to leave work daily an hour early so that I could make it to school on time. My boss told me that he admired when young people tried to make something of themselves; although I wasn't that young, I was 31.

Orientation was torture. We had to fill out a bunch of paperwork, go down to the school store and buy uniforms and carry a huge bag of school supplies that consisted of styling tools, "baby doll heads", and heavy books. I started to wonder if I had made the right choice. Besides I was one of the oldest students in the class. Most of my classmates were 18 and 19 who lived at home with their parents and had no jobs. You would think that they would be full of more life, but instead they were always tired and complaining about all the reading and writing they had to do. They came to beauty school to do hair, not to read and write. Overall, it was funny how it appeared that the younger they were, the lazier they appeared to be.

School was school, work was work, motherhood was motherhood, and church was church. The Magic Man had his surgery and we all found out that his tumor was malignant and he went fast. His death was quick and shocking. But what gave me peace was one day I was at the hospital to visit him, never really thinking that he would die. I remembered that my dad wasn't a spiritual man so I needed to know where he stood with God. I asked everyone to give me a little personal time with my dad so we could talk. I talked to him a little about God and told him that I really wanted him to be saved. I explained to him how simple it was to be saved and asked him if he wanted to give it a try. He just looked at me as if to shout "YES!" I walked him through the sinner's prayer and asked him if he believe that Christ died for his sins and if he believed it in his heart, and because he had tubes everywhere I told him to flick his thumb if the answer was yes and he flicked his thumb for yes. I told my father that he was saved and to not be afraid of death and he flicked his thumb again to let me know that he wasn't afraid.

My days were long, and some other days unbearable, but

Recognize

I was determined not to give up. My school hours were from 5pm until 10pm, Tuesdays through Fridays, and 9am until 5pm on Saturdays. During my lunch period I would tell bible stories to my classmates. They all were fascinated in hearing about the power of God. I spent every evening bringing drama to Noah's Ark and the battle between Moses and Pharaoh's army. I told them the story of Jacob and the favor he had for his son Joseph, and the story of Esther being in a beauty pageant, and David and Goliath. Each night I had a different story, and many of the girls wanted me to pray that they make it through beauty school and for other issues that they were dealing with. After a while, my storytelling became the norm and the girls looked forward to story time.

One evening, I was in the cafeteria waiting for the rest of the girls so that I could get to what had turned into a bible study, but no one showed up. I ate instead and returned to the salon floor. As I looked around no one would look at me. It was as though I did something wrong. I didn't say anything to anyone, I just let the night pass by. The next evening was a repeat, and this went on for about two weeks. One evening I waited until everyone was out of the cafeteria and spoke with a young girl named Tammy. She was very jumpy and nervous, and wanted to speak quickly. She said, "We can't talk to you, or listen to anymore of your bible stories. We were told that if we keep listening to your bible stories that something bad would happen to us." I asked, "Who told you this?" She said, "If I tell you, please, please, please don't say nothing or say that I told you." I promised her that I wouldn't. She then said, "Minnie, the girl from the islands with the Jamaican accent said that she hates your bible stories and that she is a voo doo witch, and if she burns a black candle with your name on it something bad could happen to you, so we stopped listening to your bible stories because she burned a black candle on Sandy and Sandy lost her student loan and had to drop out of school."

I was not happy about this news, and I knew that my God was able to crush the workings and activities of black candle burnings. So, I went home and prayed and asked God what I should do. The next day while everyone was eating their lunch in silence, I stood up on one of the lunch tables to make an announcement. And yes, Minnie was in attendance. "It was brought to my attention that the reason you do not attend my bible classes anymore is that Minnie frightened you with a threat to burn a black candle with your name on it. Minnie operates with the power of Satan and I operate with the power of God. Just like the story of Moses that we talked about when Mose's snake ate the snake of Pharaoh's men, so will my God's power overtake the power of voodoo." Minnie stood up in the middle of the cafeteria and announced that she would burn four candles with my name on them and prove that all that stuff that they'd been learning about my so-call God was nothing, and that her and her black candles would win and bring me down. I rebutted with, "I send every hex and vex back to you 100 fold with the power and authority of Jesus Christ."

The girls just watched in silence. Everyone went home as if it was a normal night. Fear tried to set in but I rebuked it and prayed over myself and family and spoke to God and my ministering angels to cover me with the precious blood of Jesus Christ. I went to sleep with the peace of God. The next day everyone was looking at me as if I was supposed to be missing a body part or something, and Minnie was watching me very closely as well. This went on for about a week and

Recognize

nothing out of the norm happened.

One day about six days later, Minnie's roommate who was also a student at the beauty school came running into the school out of breath saying that they just got burned out and Minnie's son was hurt in the fire. I couldn't hear what was going on because none of the girls were speaking to me out of fear. Than the next day, her roommate came running in late for class because Minnie's car was repossessed due to non-payment. About a week later, Minnie was in the school office taking care of some business. She saw me but looked away. I found out later that she had to drop out of school because she lost her job and couldn't continue to pay for school. Within a two-week timeframe she was burned out, lost a lot of her personal items, had an injured boy, lost her car, job, and had to drop out of beauty school. I guess these tragedies were aimed at me, but my God who is all powerful lifted up a standard against my enemy. Every candle she burned with my name on it was pointed toward her.

About a week later, I was sitting by myself eating a sandwich and one of the girls came over to ask me to tell her a bible story. I was shocked and held back my smile. She said, "All the girls want you to start back telling bible stories and sent me over here to ask you. We know that Minnie burned candles with your name on them and nothing happened to you, but everything happened to her. We want to know more about God."

We were back to our old routine and all was well. After about five months, I saw Minnie at the school. It looked like she was being reinstated. We just looked at each other without a word. I was hoping that she wasn't there to start any trouble, but I did believe that she recognized that my God was a powerful God and had more power than her black candles. She was back in school, and during our lunch hour I saw her watching how things were back to normal. I would be in an area with a large crowd listening to my bible stories, and she would be in a little corner eating by herself. I knew what that felt like and wanted to offer her salvation or even just to sit with the rest of us, but I had to pray about it first. The girls were treating Minnie as if she had a disease. I went home and prayed that God would open up a door for me to minister to her and to show her that I didn't hate her, but instead that I loved her with the love of Christ.

We were on the salon floor one day and were being graded on finger waves. Minnie could never get hers right. I walked over to her and showed her where she was going wrong, and if she adjusted her fingers, she could get the style right. She was shocked that I had taken the time to show her. I could hear the teacher as she walked and graded each student as the room was very quiet because everyone was working hard to get a good grade. I had a clear view of Minnie when the teacher approached her. "Great improvement Minnie," the teacher said, and Minnie looked over at me with a smile, I smiled back.

That evening during bible study, or story time as the girls called it, I asked Minnie if she wanted to come over, and she picked up her lunch and we all made room for her on the bench. She was full of questions and everyone was happy that the stories they'd been hearing for months were just as powerful in real life as in the bible days. To God Be The Glory!

Recognize

A PRAYER TO REPAIR THE WORK OF THE ENEMY

Father God I come to You as humbly as I know how. I repent for all known and unknown sins, and I renounce any and all occults, witchcraft, and ungodly activities that may have made its way into my life. I break every ungodly soul tie in my life, and cast out fear right now in the mighty Name of Jesus. Jesus Christ of Nazareth I have accepted You as my Lord and Savior and will have no other gods before You. Lord, by faith I believe I am healed by Your stripes. I am healed in my mind, my emotions, and in every other area in my life that needs repair. I am a new creation in You and all old things are truly passed away. I pray that my ministering angels, comforting angel, and guarding angel are with me day in and day out. I know that I am Your child, and that You are my Lord, and with You, all things are possible, and without You, I'm nothing. Lord Thank You for delivering me, healing, me and loving me. In Jesus Name, AMEN!

CONCLUSION

In everyone's life, some rain must fall, but it's time for us to recognize the difference between rain, life's growing pains and curses or demonic forces that are operating in our lives. Satan and his team live in the spirit realm and he (being the adversary) knows who you are. Sometimes before you are even aware of whom you are. Therefore, Satan set out to destroy you as early in life as possible. The more powerful you become in the things of God, the more he will try to destroy you by using the simple things in life. I'm a living witness that the more God uses you, the more you have to be on the watch. The Word of God says "watch" as well as pray.

I have seen more underground activity while writing this book than ever before. There were so many hinderances in writing this book; reason being is I believe that you (the reader) are being set free in this hour and God is changing your mindset so that He can put you into position to do kingdom work. The more your eyes are opened to the things of the Spirit, the more God can use you. Please remember that the price was already paid on Calvary over 2,000 years ago. In Isaiah 53:5 it says "But He was wounded for our transgressions, He was bruised for our iniquities; the chastisement for our peace was upon Him, and by His stripes we are healed."

Sharing my experience with you through God's anointing is apart of my ministry to set the captive free. You may have recognized from reading this book some areas in your life where Satan may be operating but you have the authority to bind him and loose the peace of God over your life. My

Recognize

prayers are with you and I welcome your prayers as I continue to share the secret things of God with you. The next time you are faced with anything that's not of God, all I have to say is "YOU BETTER RECOGNIZE!

Confronting the demonic forces that control our lives

About The Author

Toni Akers is an ordained minister, and a former Assistant Pastor of Commonwealth Community Church. The founder and president of a women ministry; "T.E.A. Inc.; Teaching and Equipping with an Anointing located in Chicago, Illnois. At T.E.A. she holds monthly Tea Parties for women in the Chicago area using bible principles to teach a better way of living. Women form all over Chicago and surrounding Suburbs have attended one or more of her powerful sessions. She is married to Rudy and has two children. In addition, she is a teacher, preacher, and is also gifted in the area of healing and deliverance. To add to her gift of healing, she is a certified herbalist and licensed cosmetologist. While ministering to women, she has also ministered to many men. She has appeared on TV and on several local radio stations. Toni believes that when she accepts a speaking engagement it is an assignment from God with signs and wonders following. Currently, she runs a homeless shelter for women and children, and works with churches to build their women ministries.

Reverened Akers welcomes all letters and questions. You can contact Reverened Akers via internet: www.toniakers.com